fractal fantasies

COLORING BOOK

....

25 FRACTAL DESIGNS
&
25 FRACTAL MANDALAS

....

SHEILA FREDRICKSON

Published by Etcetera Publishing, LLC 2016
First Edition

Illustrations and design © 2016 Sheila Fredrickson

ISBN 978-0-9899112-8-3

INSTRUCTIONS ...

Thanks for buying this book, and I hope you enjoy it!

May I suggest that you carefully take the book apart and separate the pages? If this is not your preference, you could also consider carefully cutting the spine off and binding the pages with spiral or wire binding. Extra room has been allowed in the center spread so the designs won't be cut or broken.

Please put a sheet of paper behind each design as you color to prevent bleed through, especially if you are using markers.

ABOUT THIS BOOK ...

Thank you again for buying this book, and exploring fractals with me!

A number of years ago, many years after my college fine arts degree was completed, I started playing with fractal software. At first I shook my head a lot and wondered why anyone would enjoy making fractals, because they were an entirely new way of thinking.

Soon I became absorbed in the lines and shapes. It was relaxing, restful, and at the end of a long day, inspirational. I began to really explore this new, creative medium I had not experienced before.

As I explored, I wondered what I might be able to do with these colorful and beautiful designs, and if anyone else might want to look at them. After several years had passed, when I often took time to either color with my children or just for my own enjoyment, it occurred to me that many of these fractal designs were colorable!

They are by no means perfect. You will likely find errors, and some designs may even make you shake your head! You will also find variety, simplicity, complexity, and the chance to make these designs your own. I tried to include a wide range of different kinds of fractal designs, and it is my hope there is something here for everyone.

The back cover of the book shows the original color versions of the fractals I used to generate the line art and mandalas. This may provide inspiration for your color choices, but don't limit yourself to my colors if you have a better idea.

Each fractal pattern is followed by a mandala made from the same fractal pattern; 25 pairs in all.

It is my hope that in these designs, you will also find joy, peace, relief from the stress of daily living, and the chance to hope and dream.

—*Sheila Fredrickson*

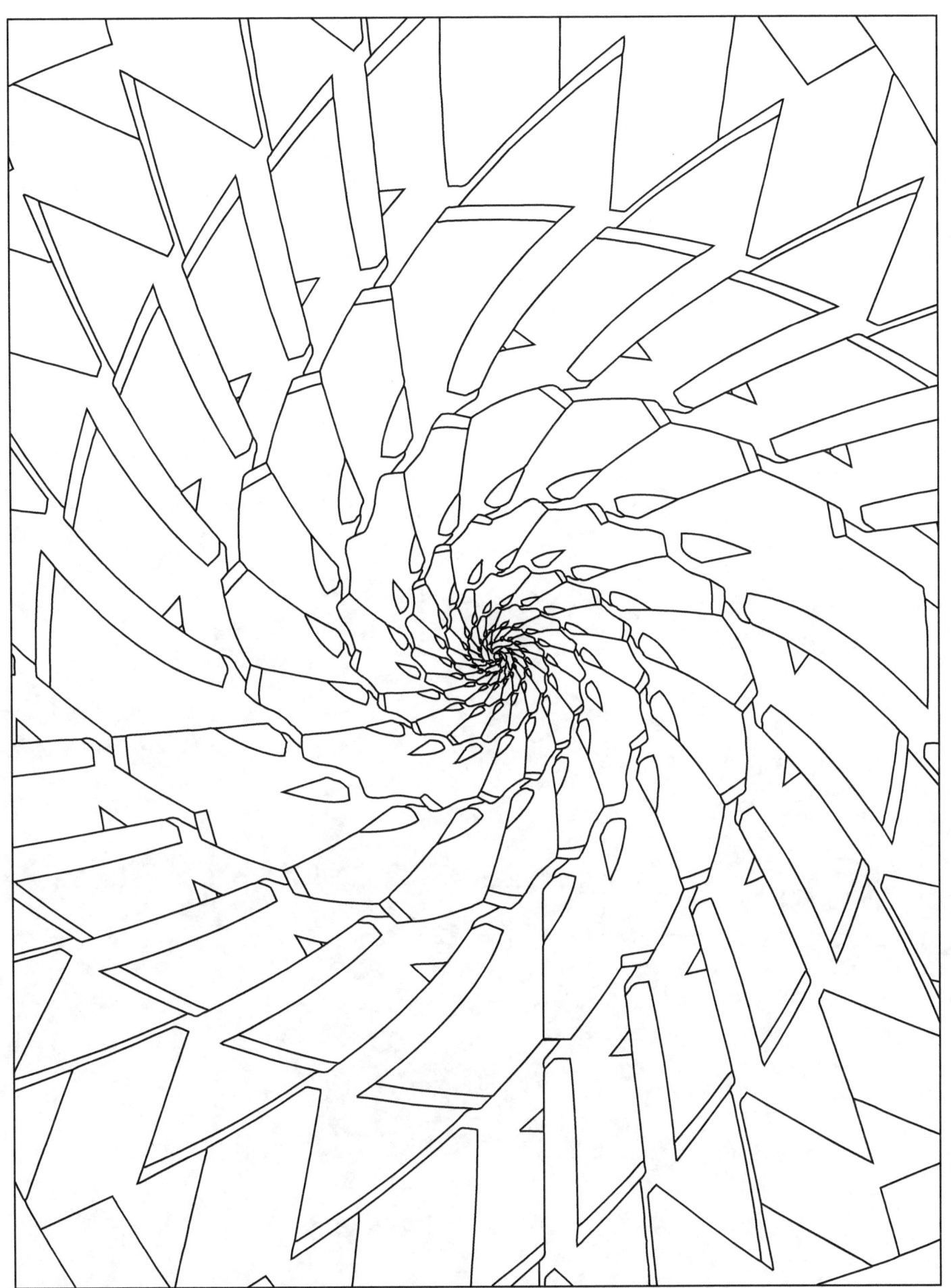

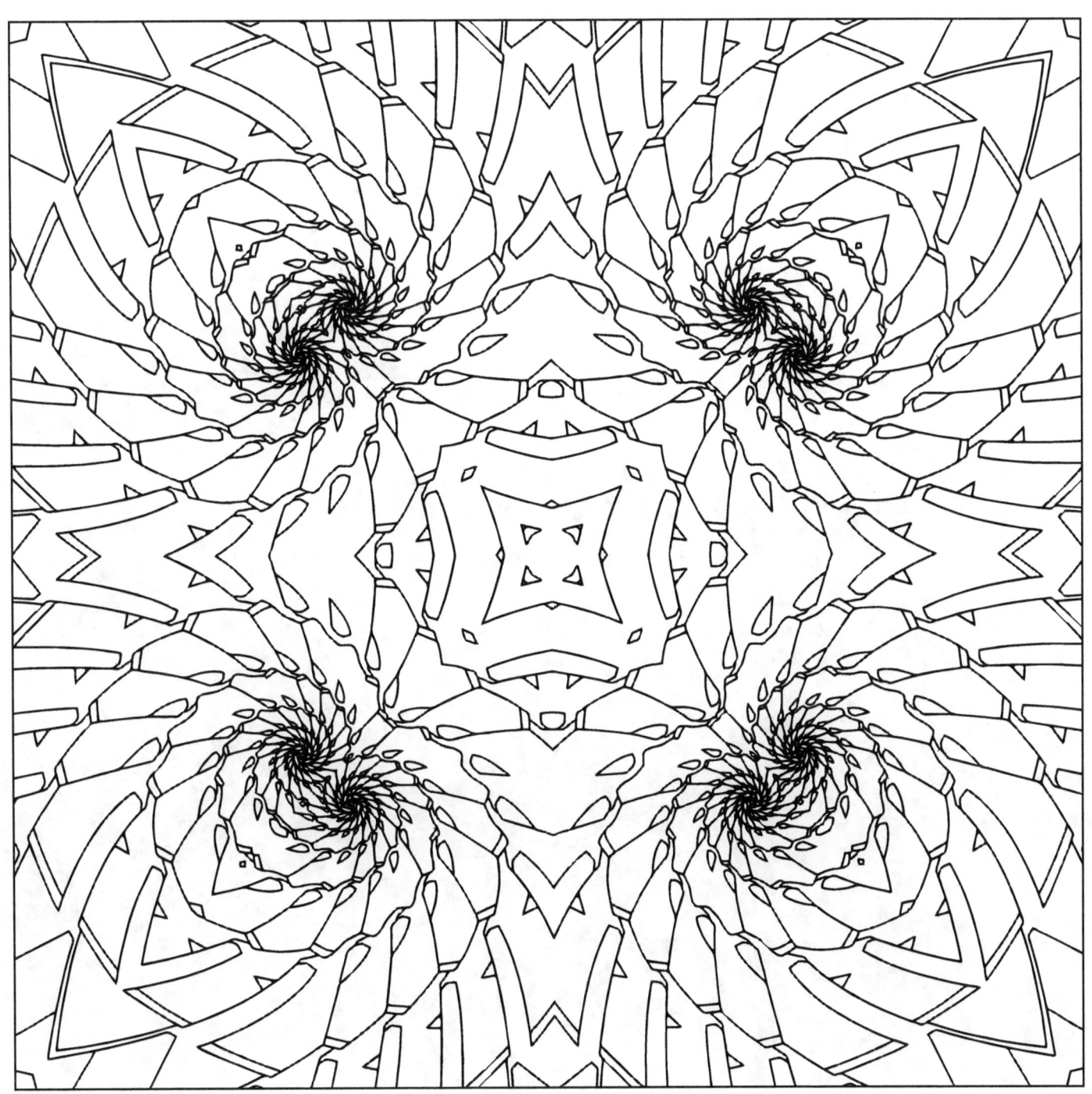

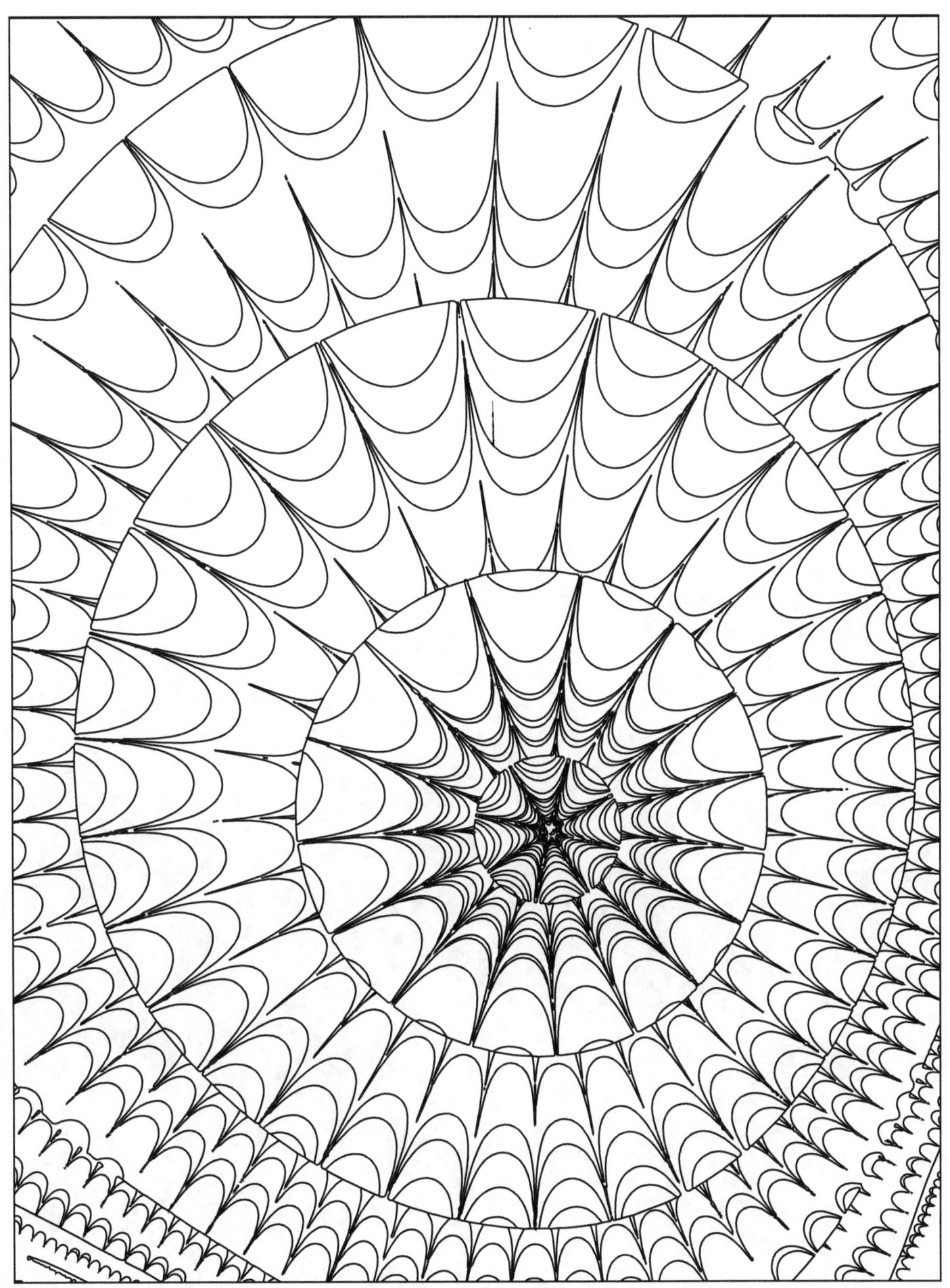

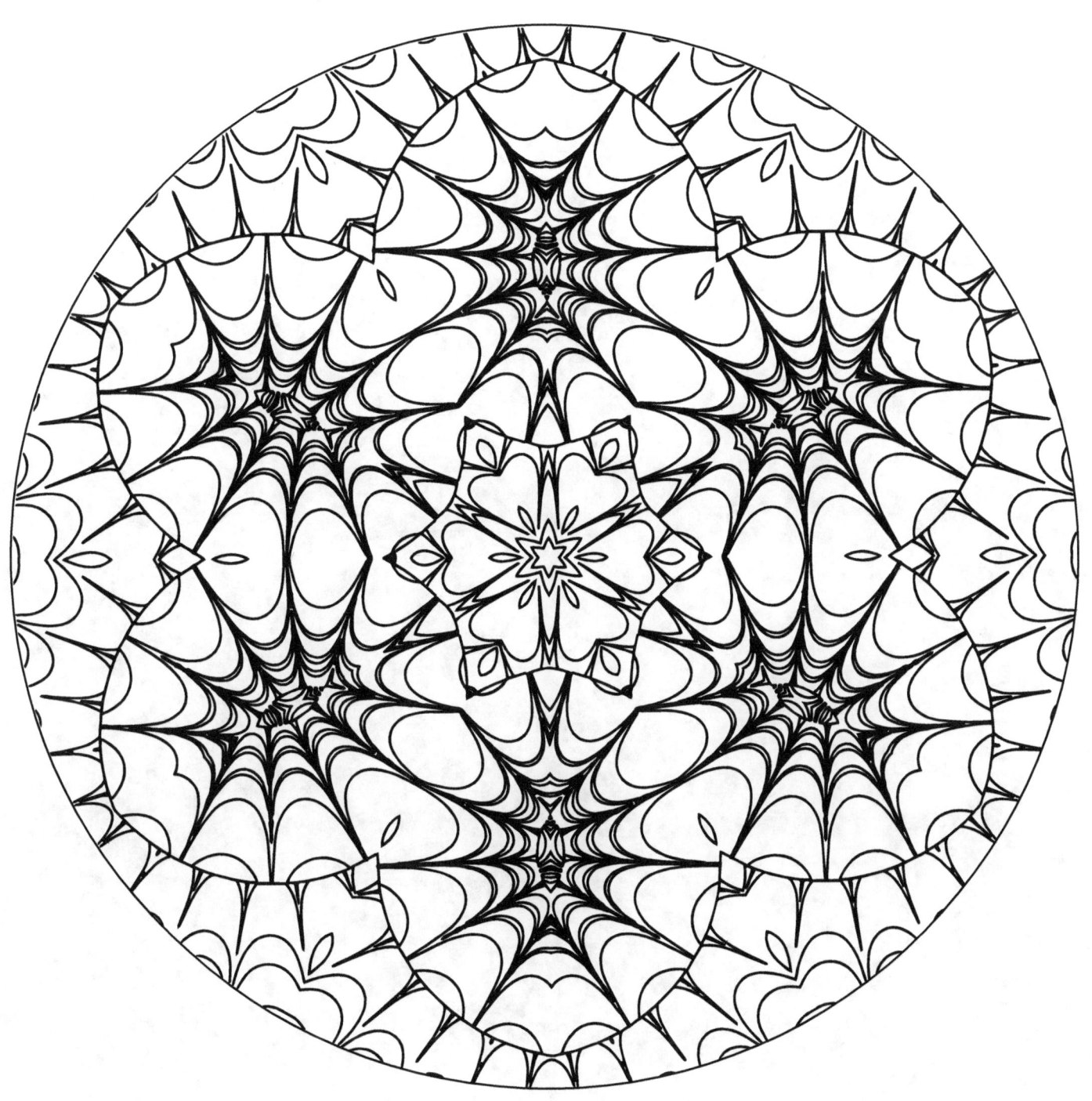

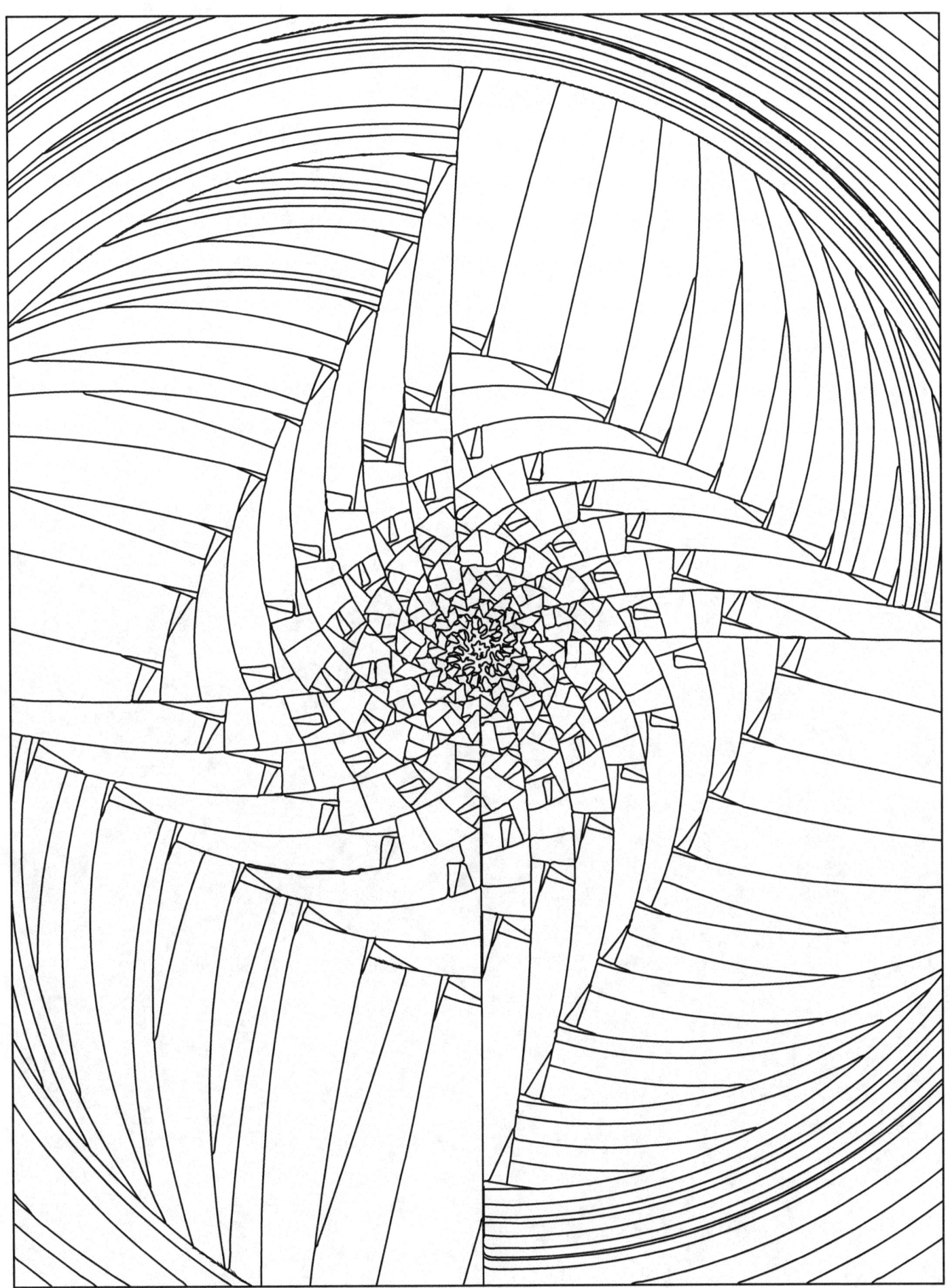

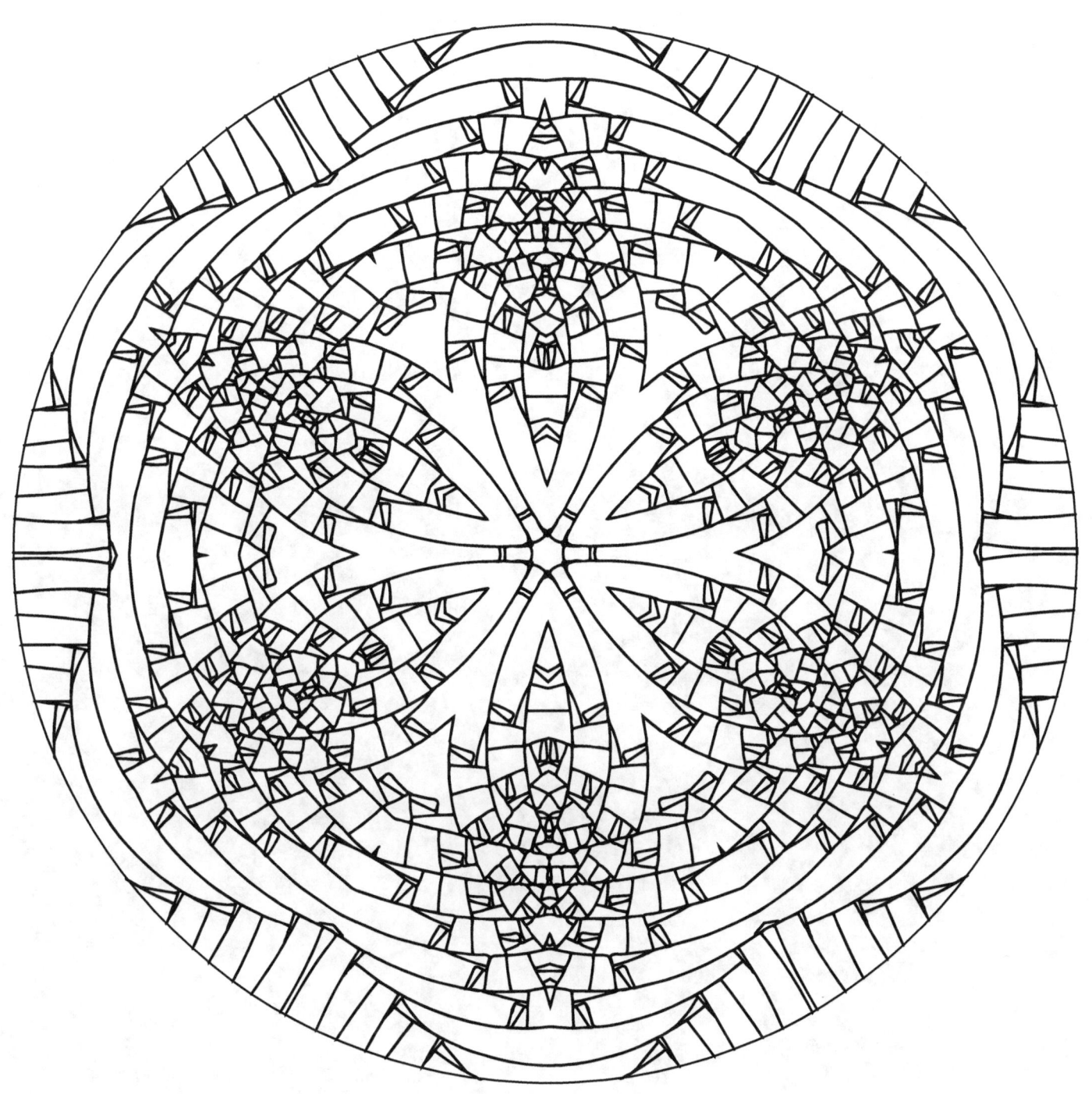

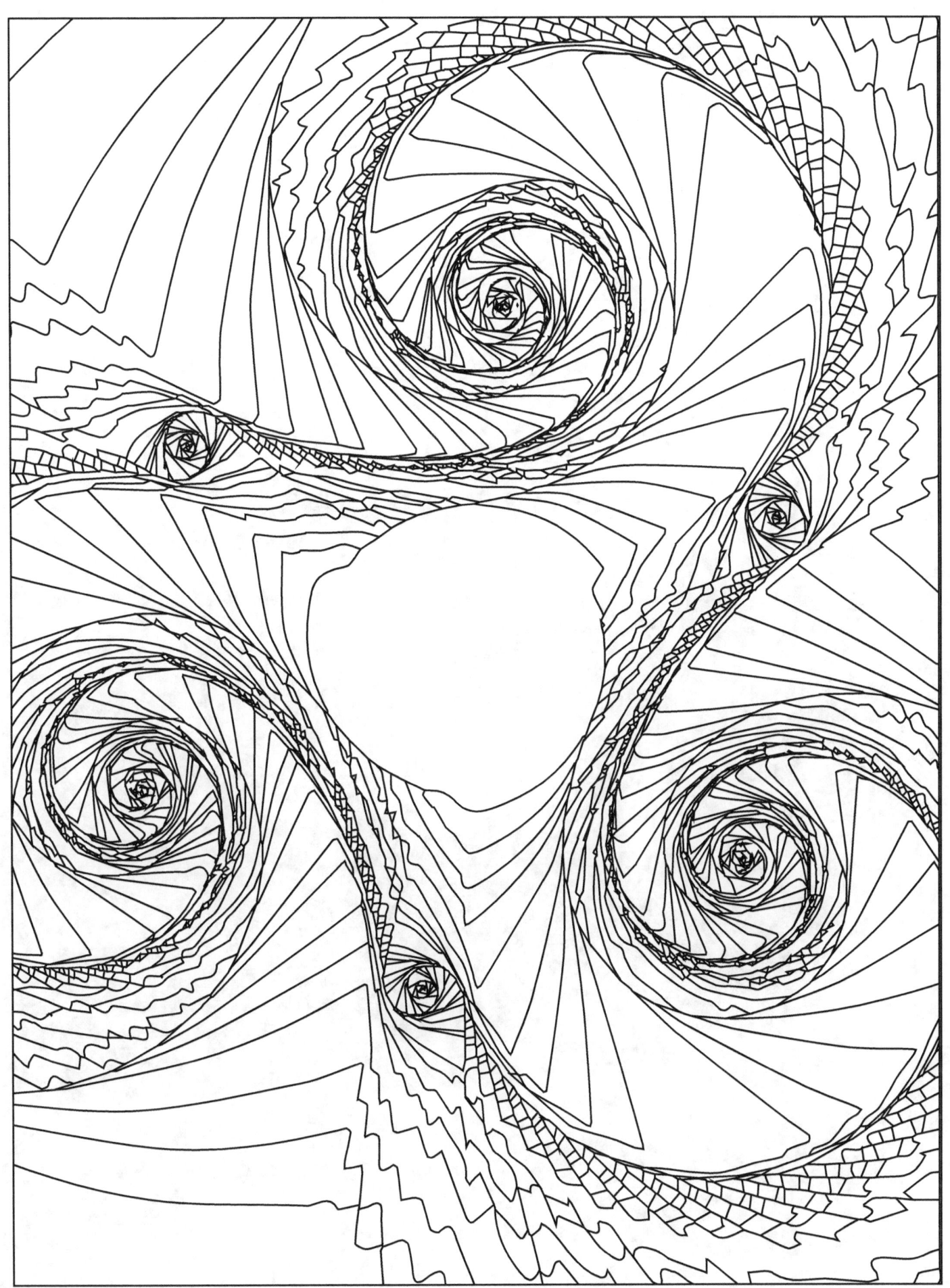

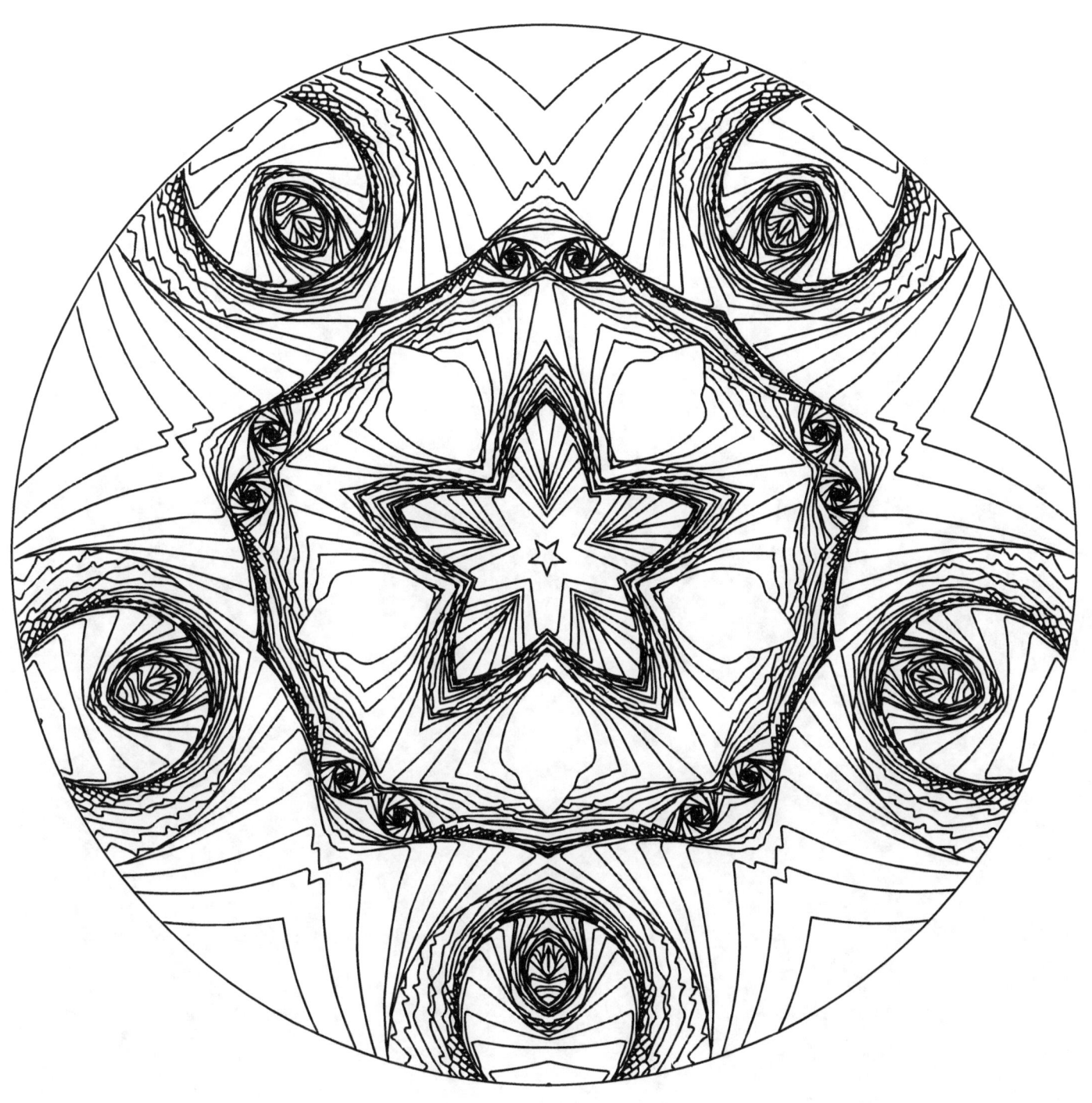

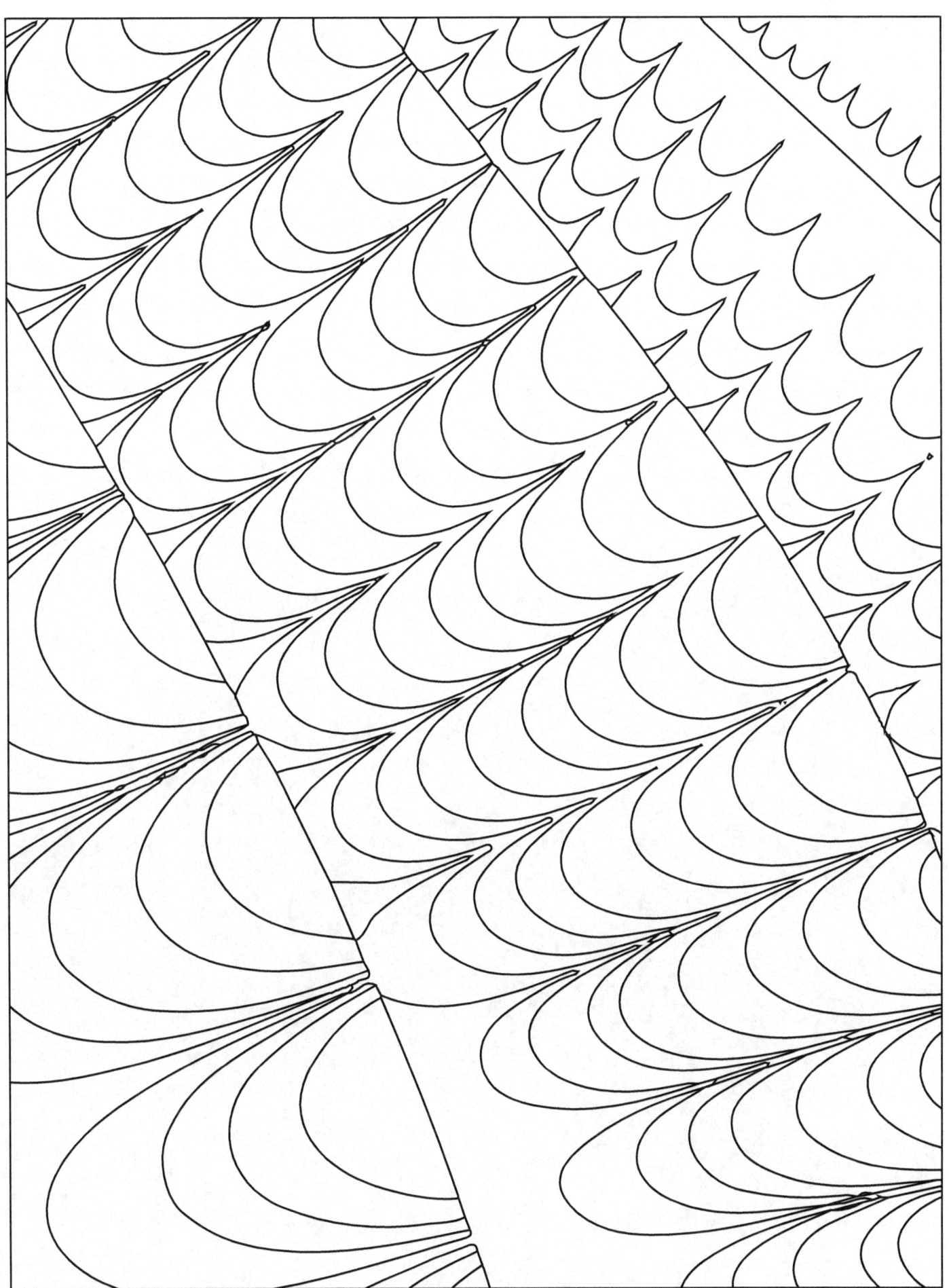

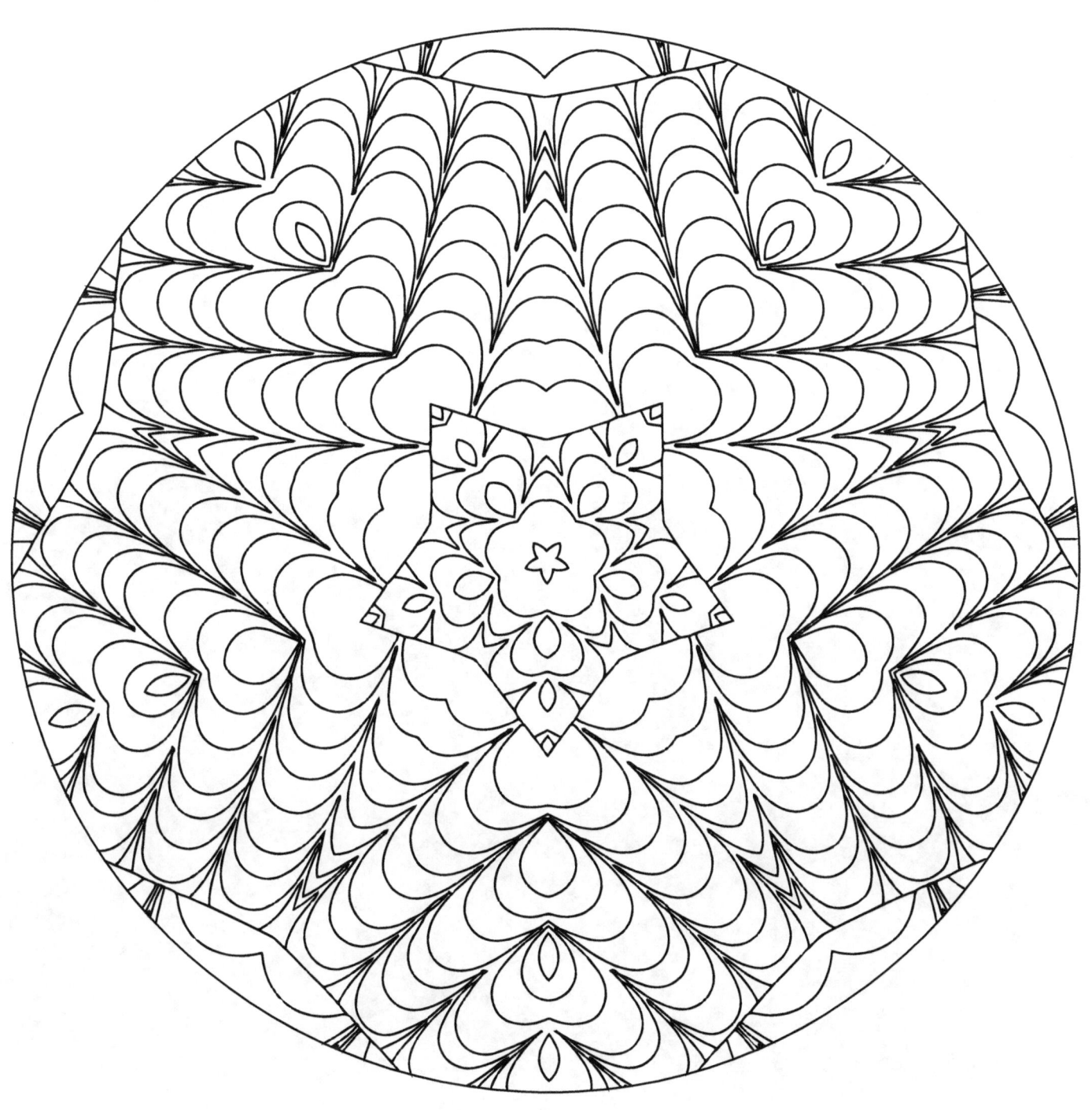

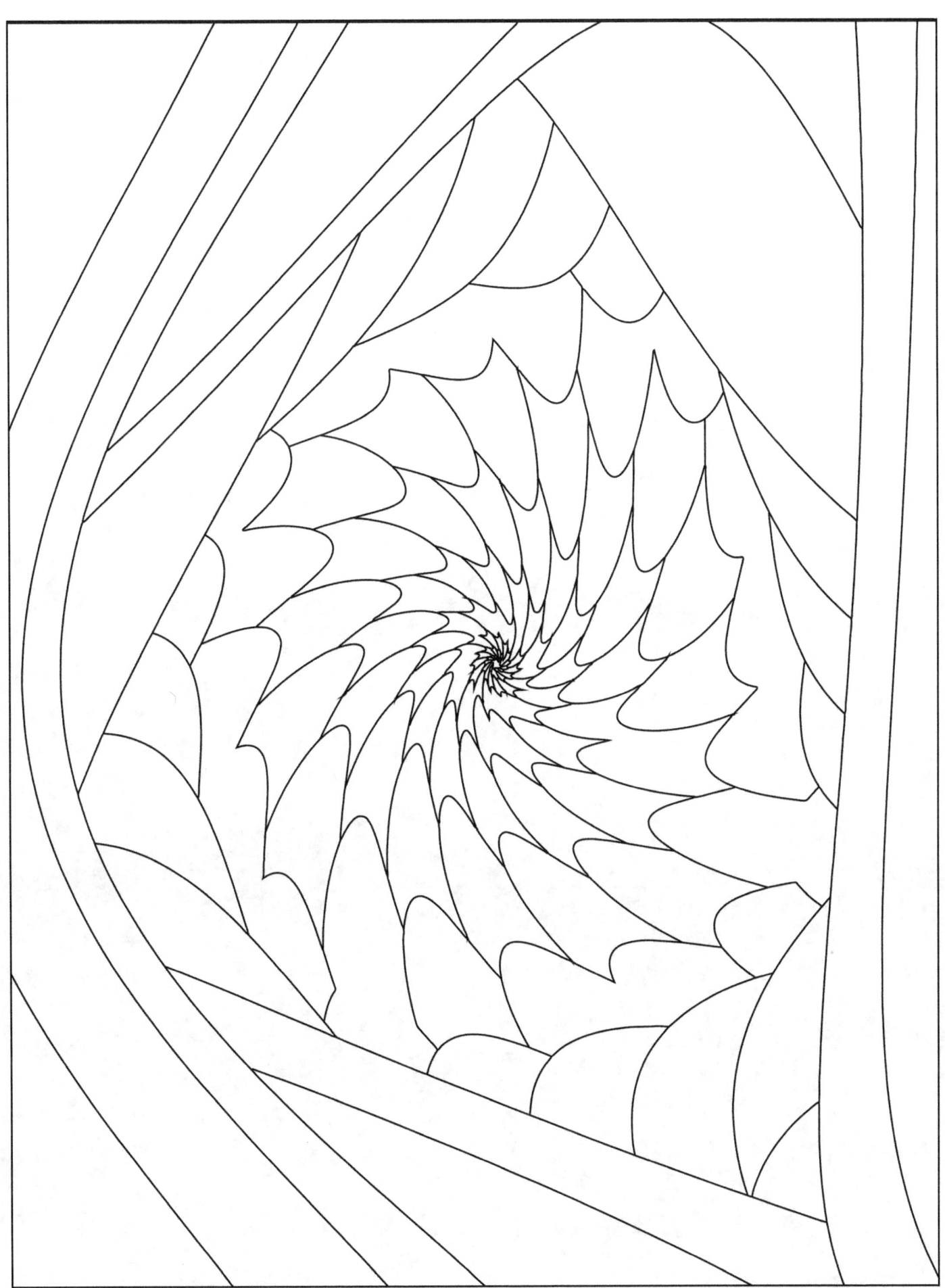

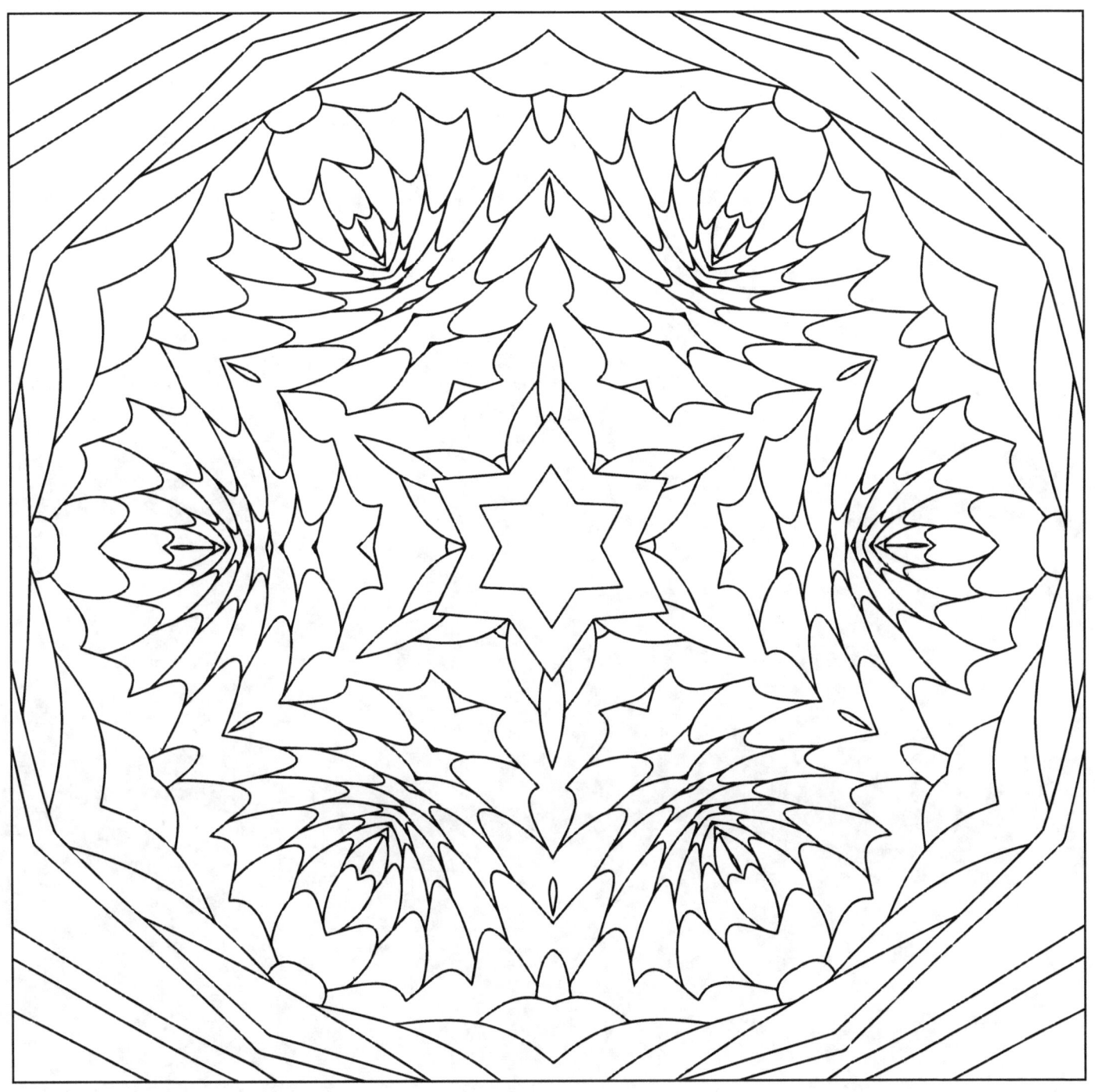

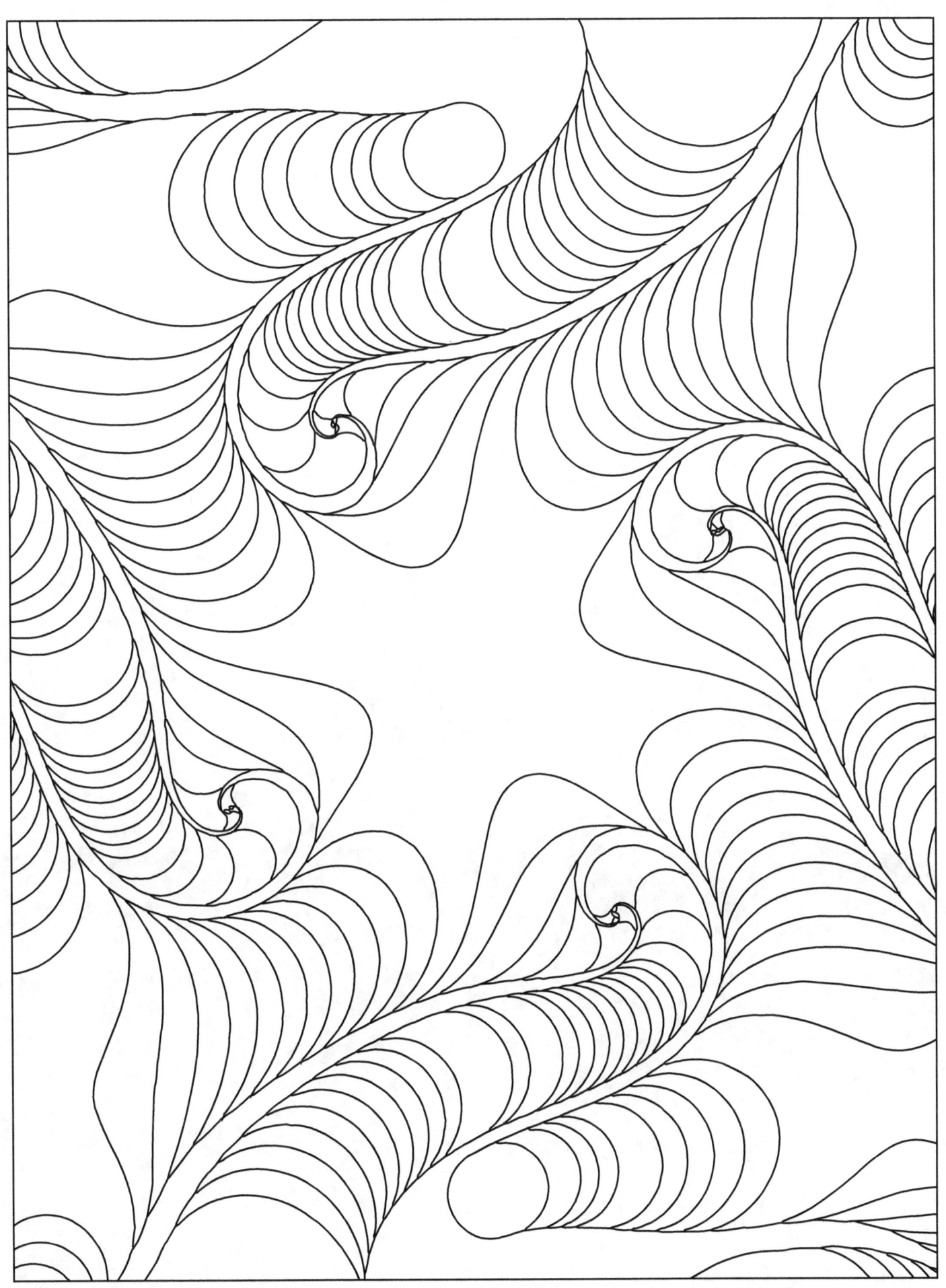

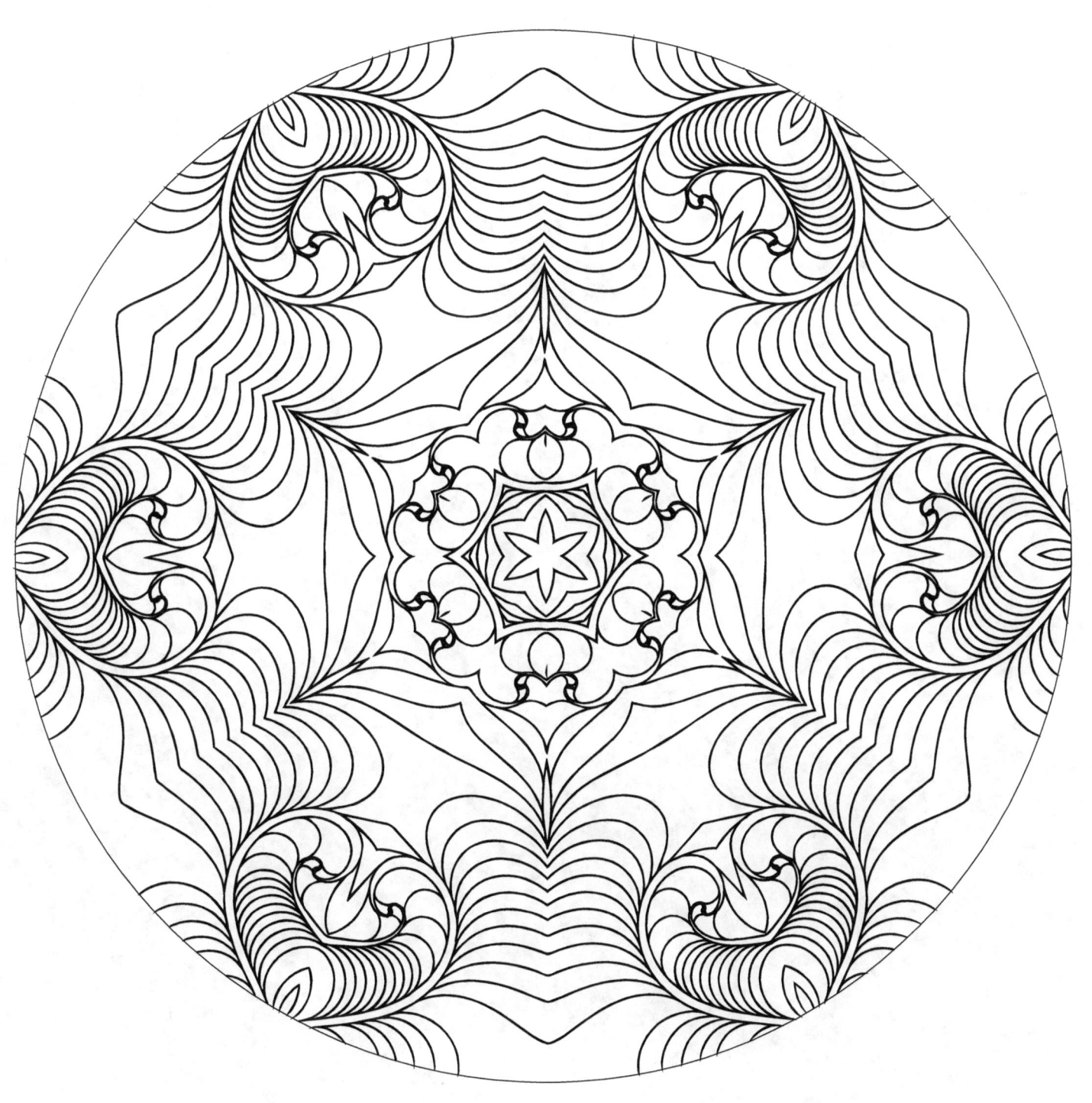

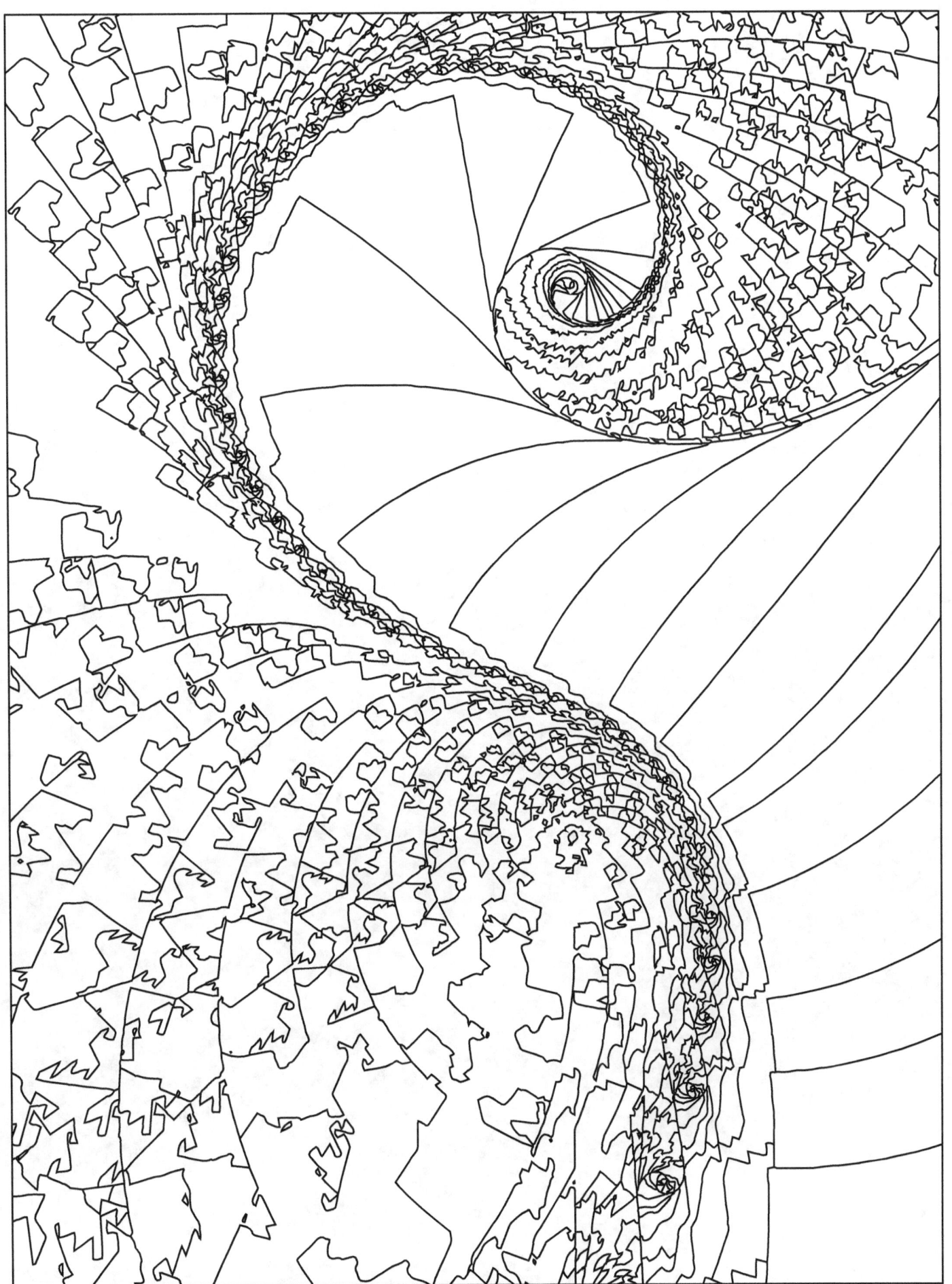

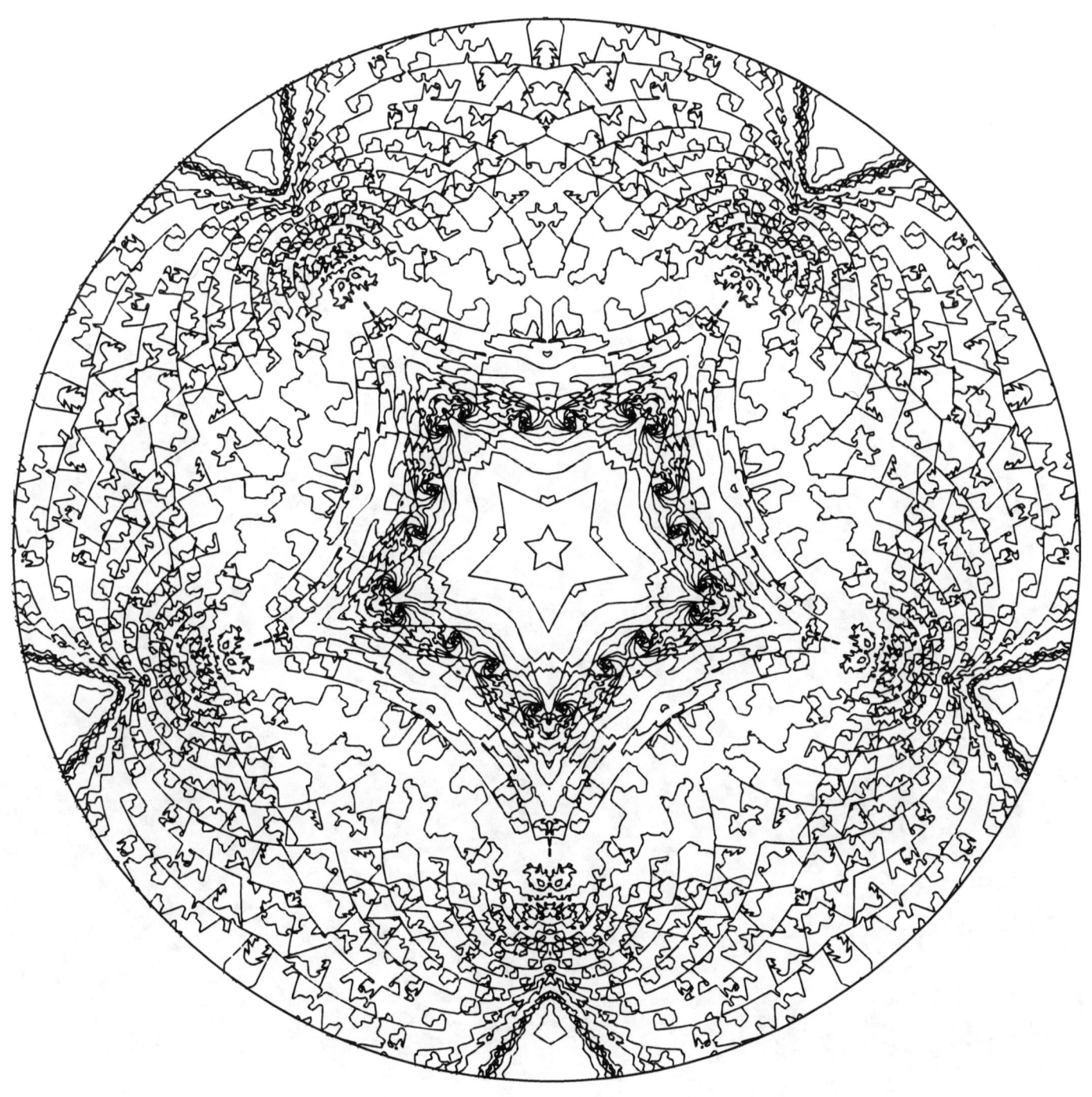

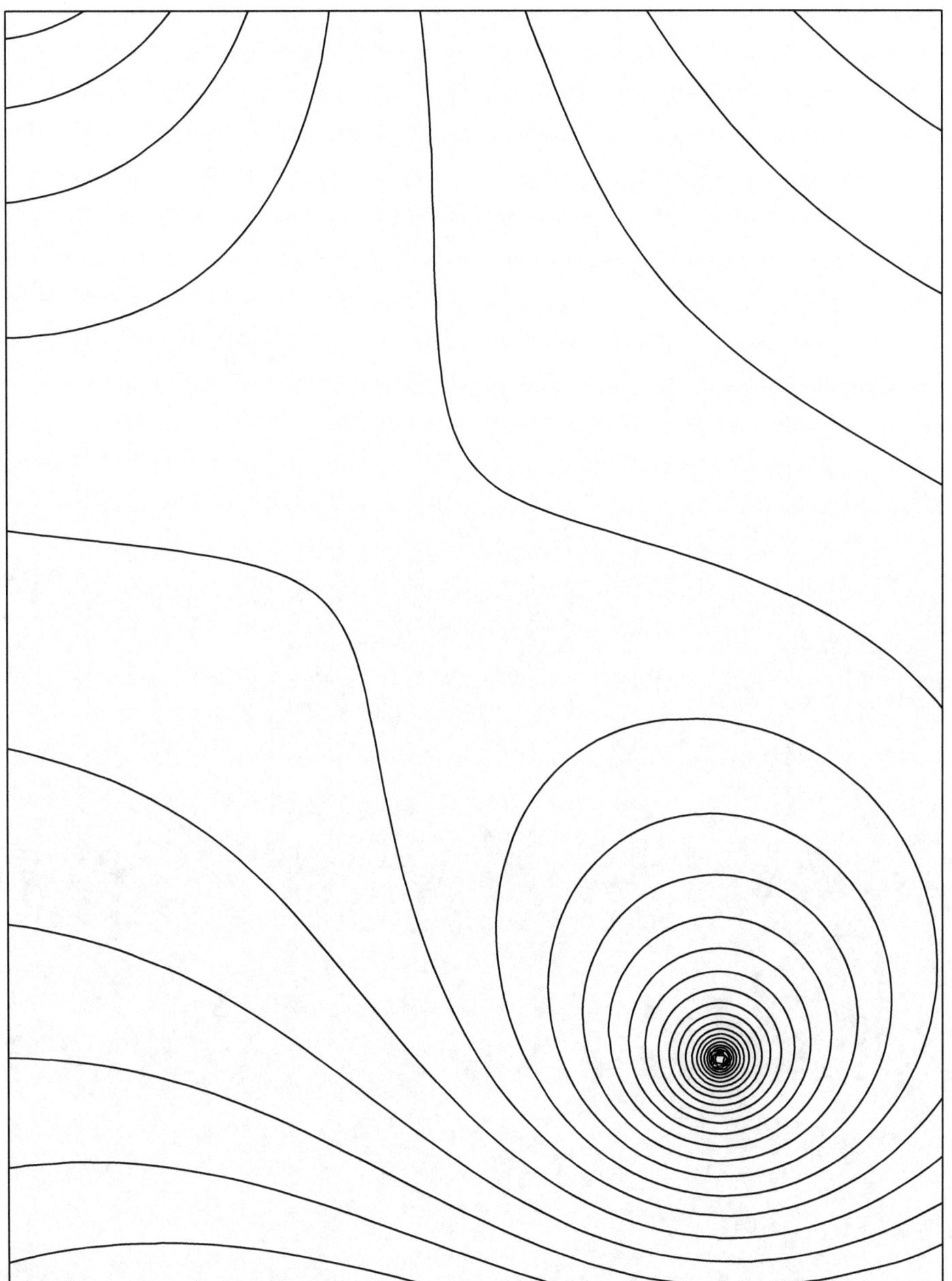

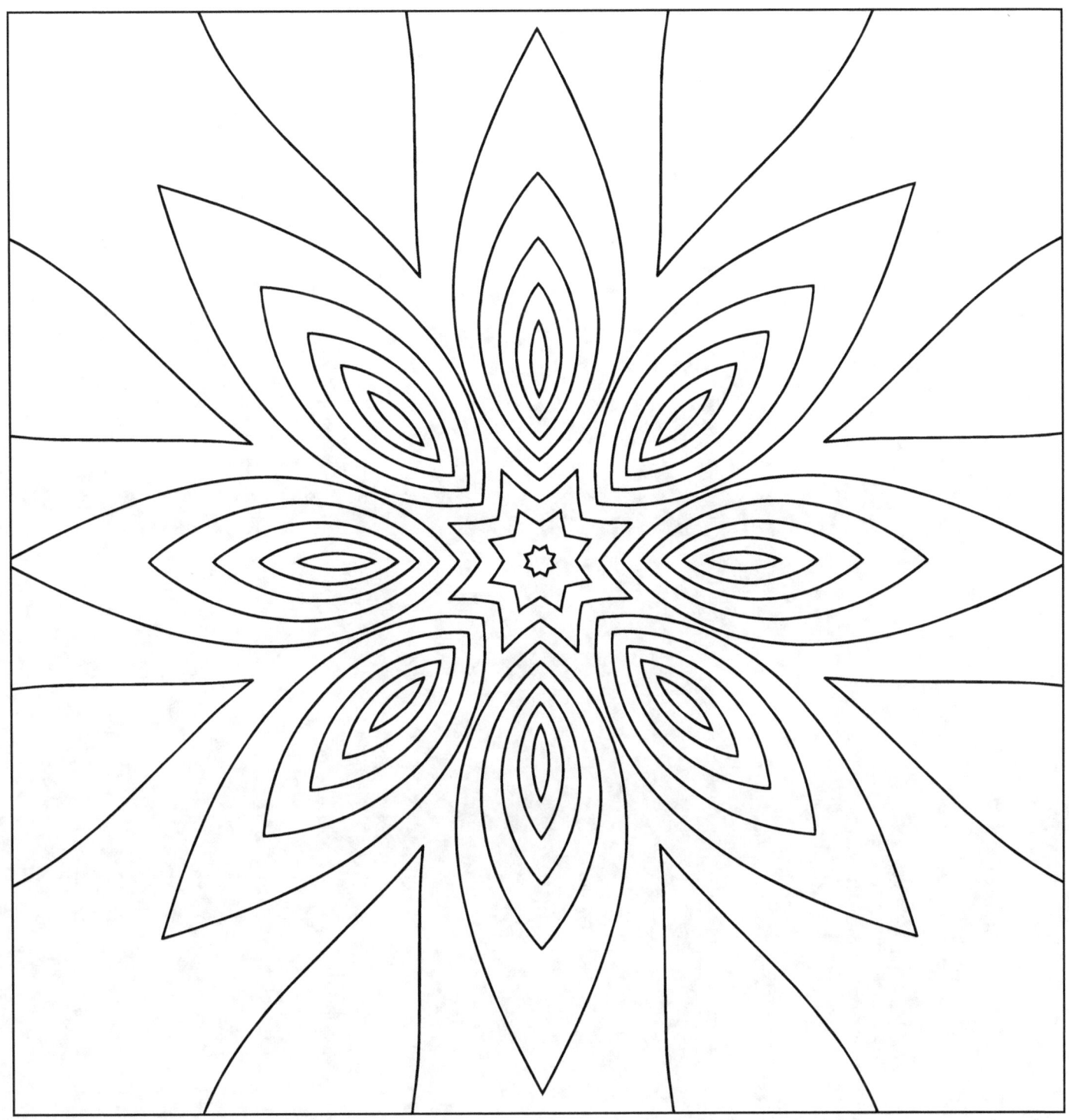

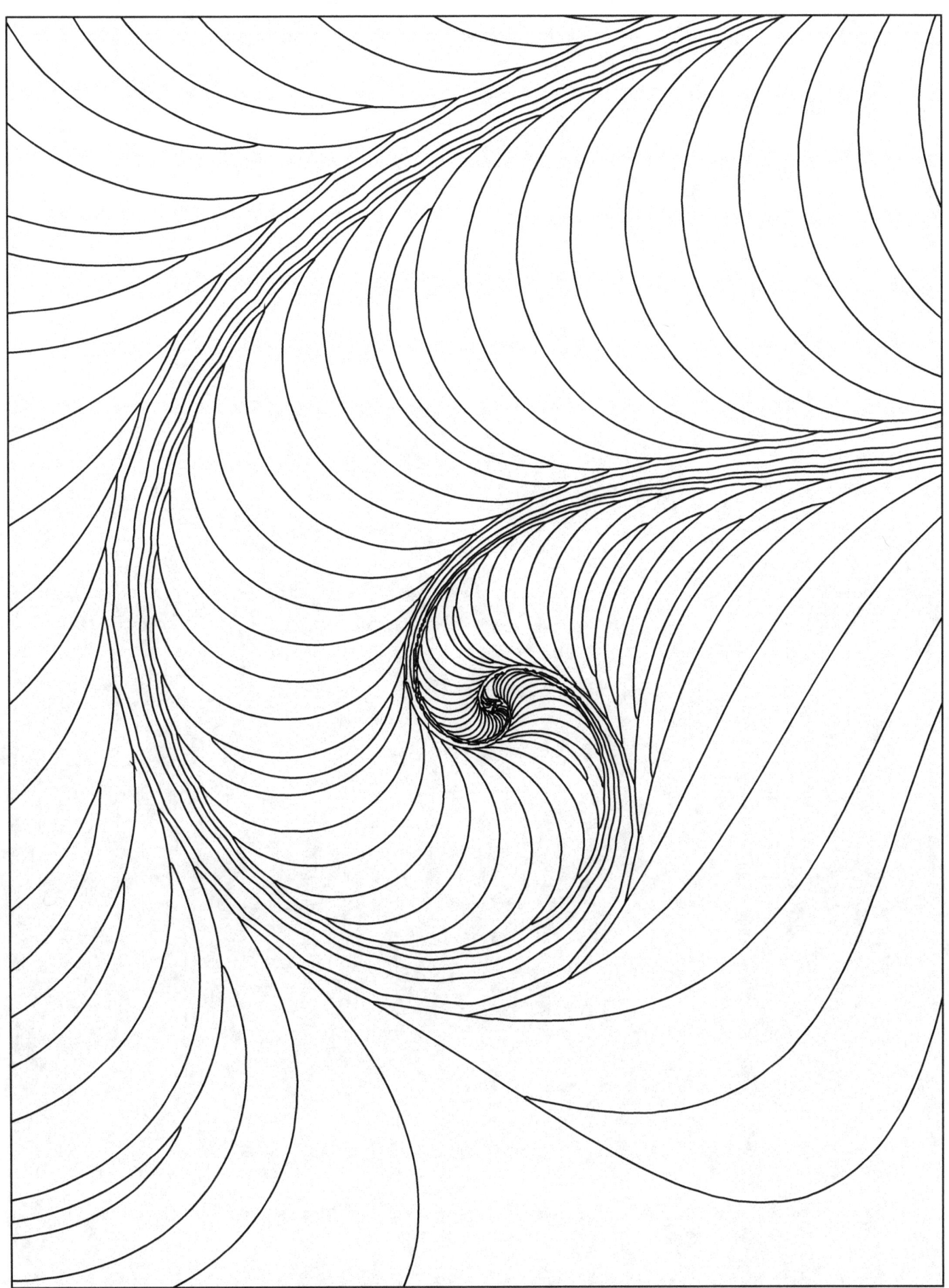

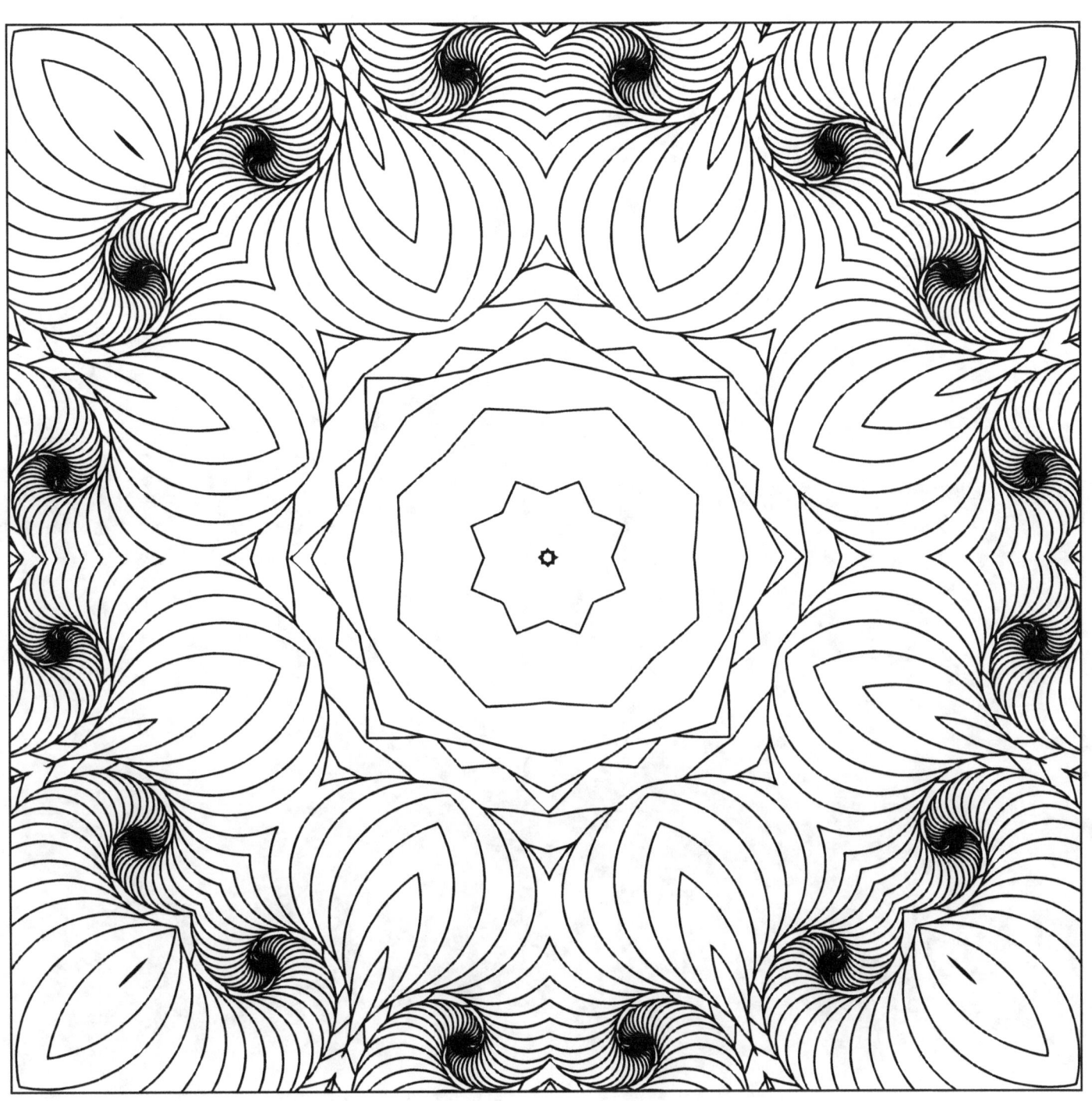

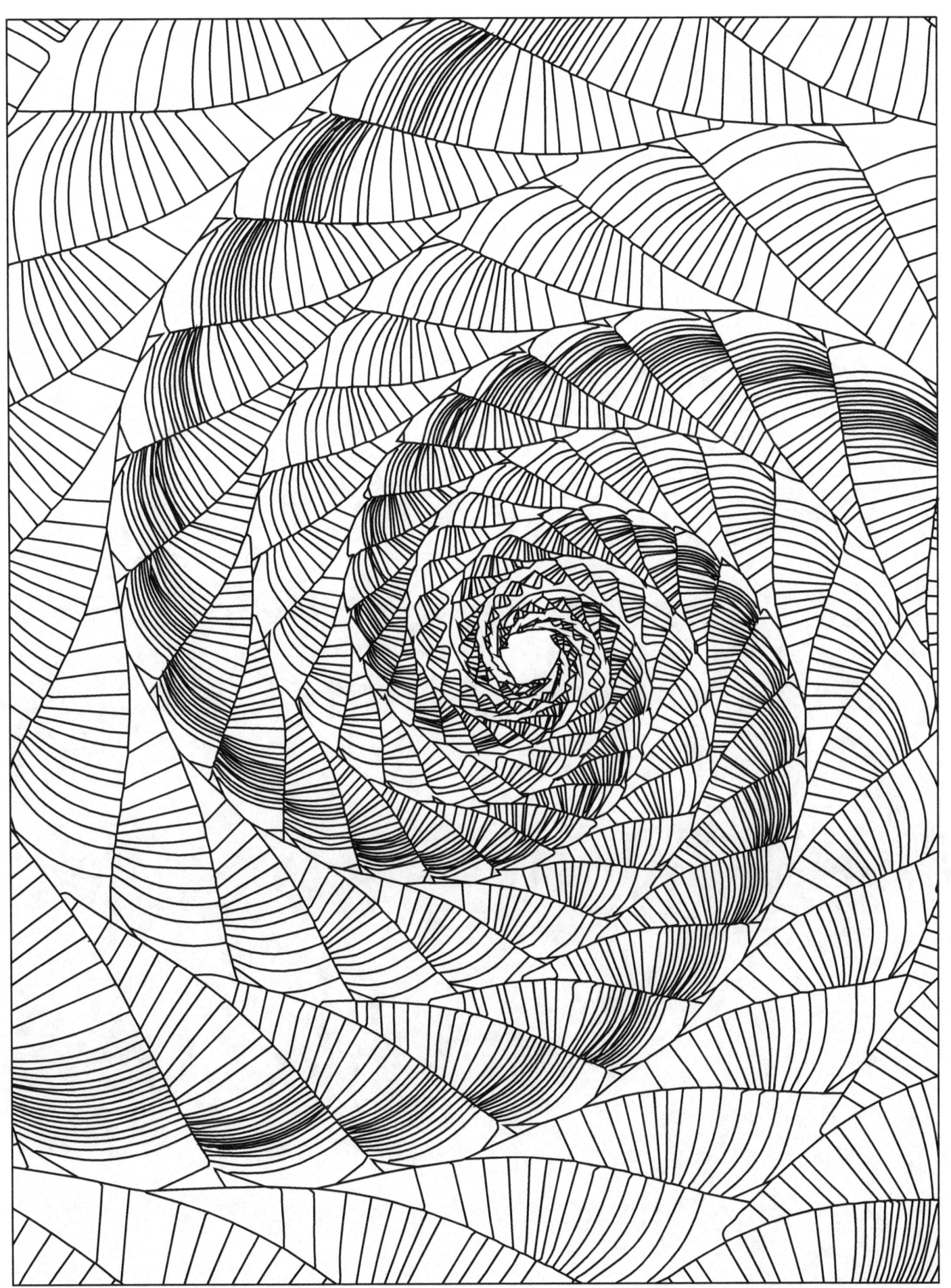

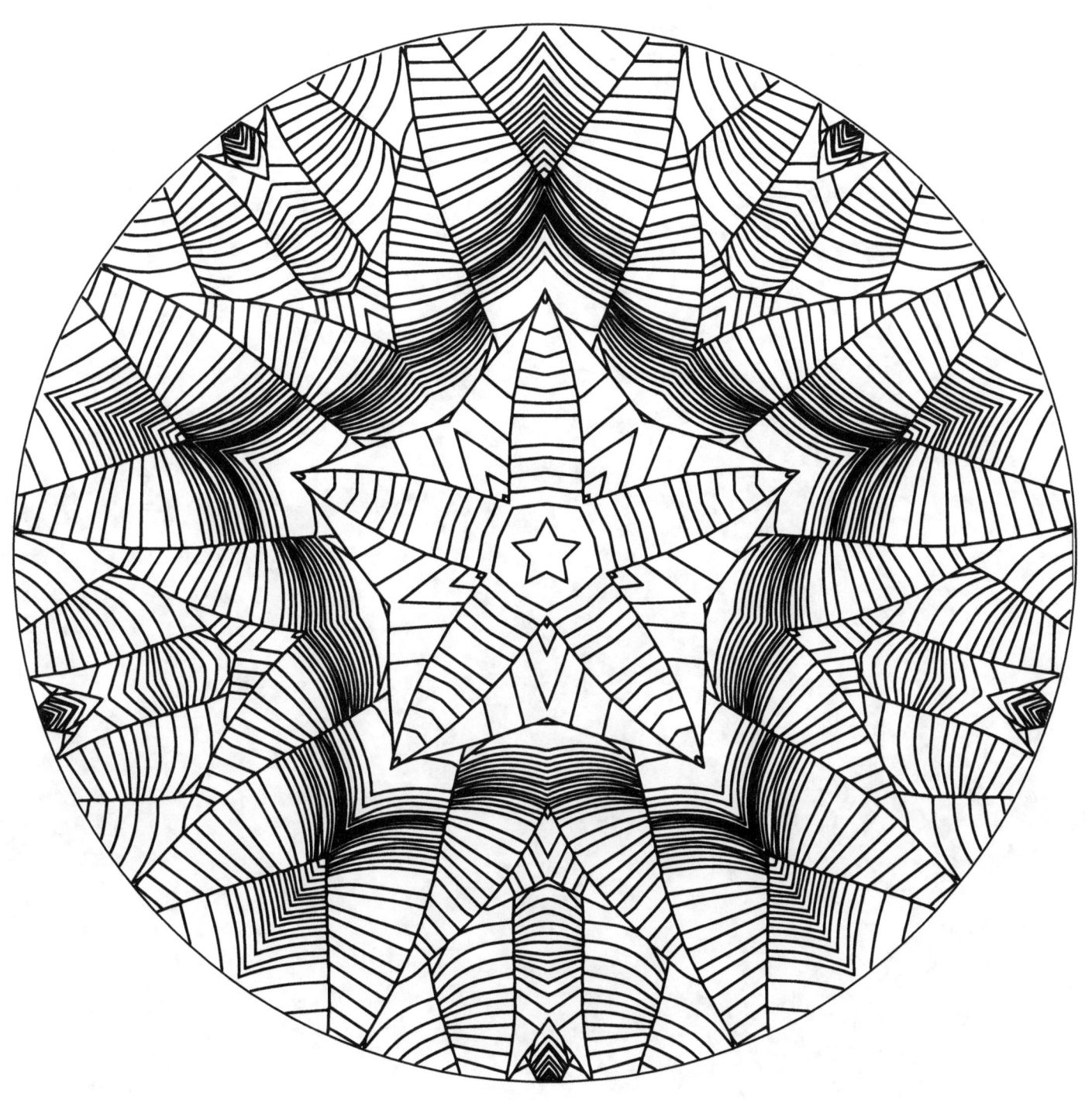

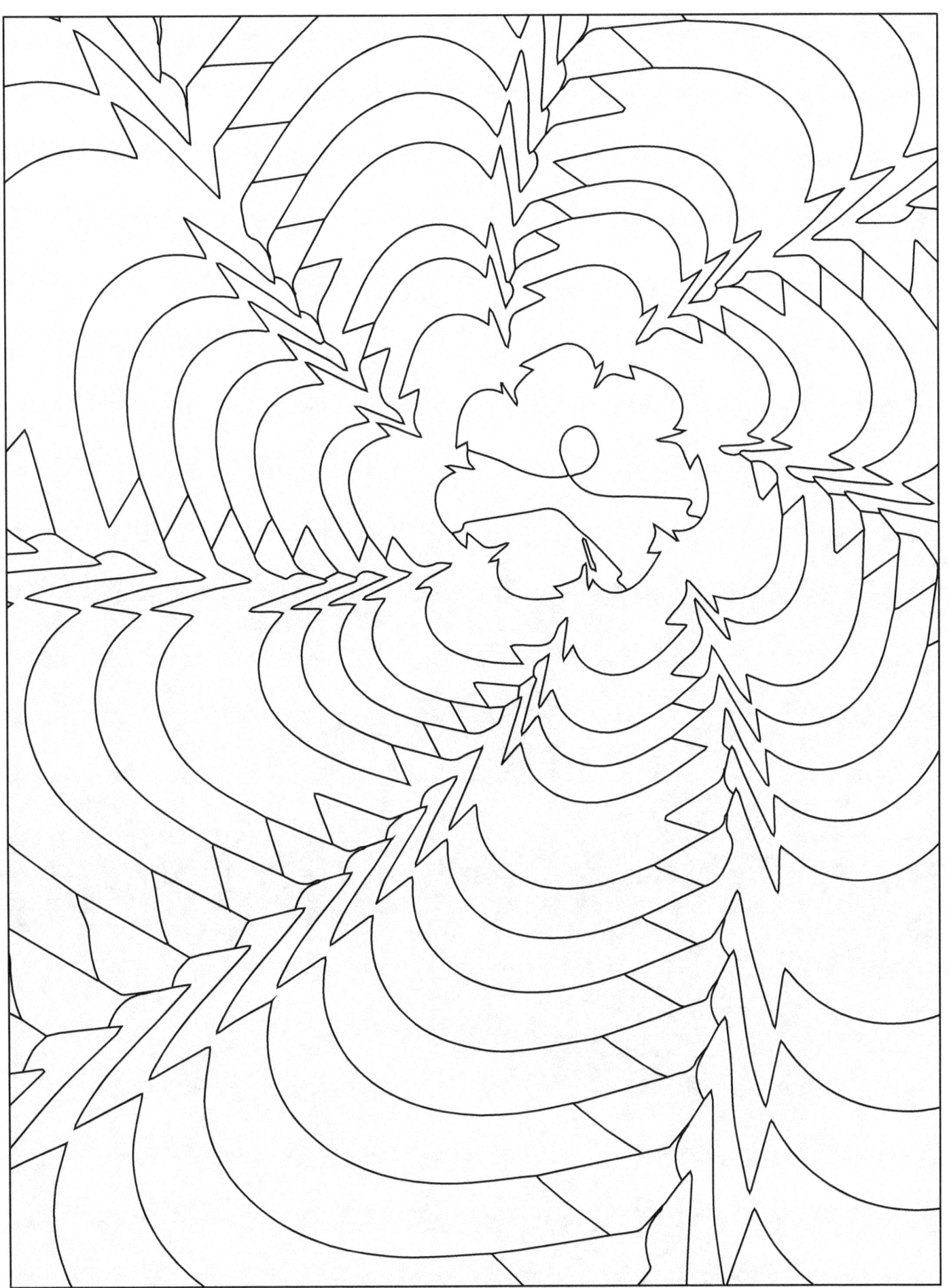

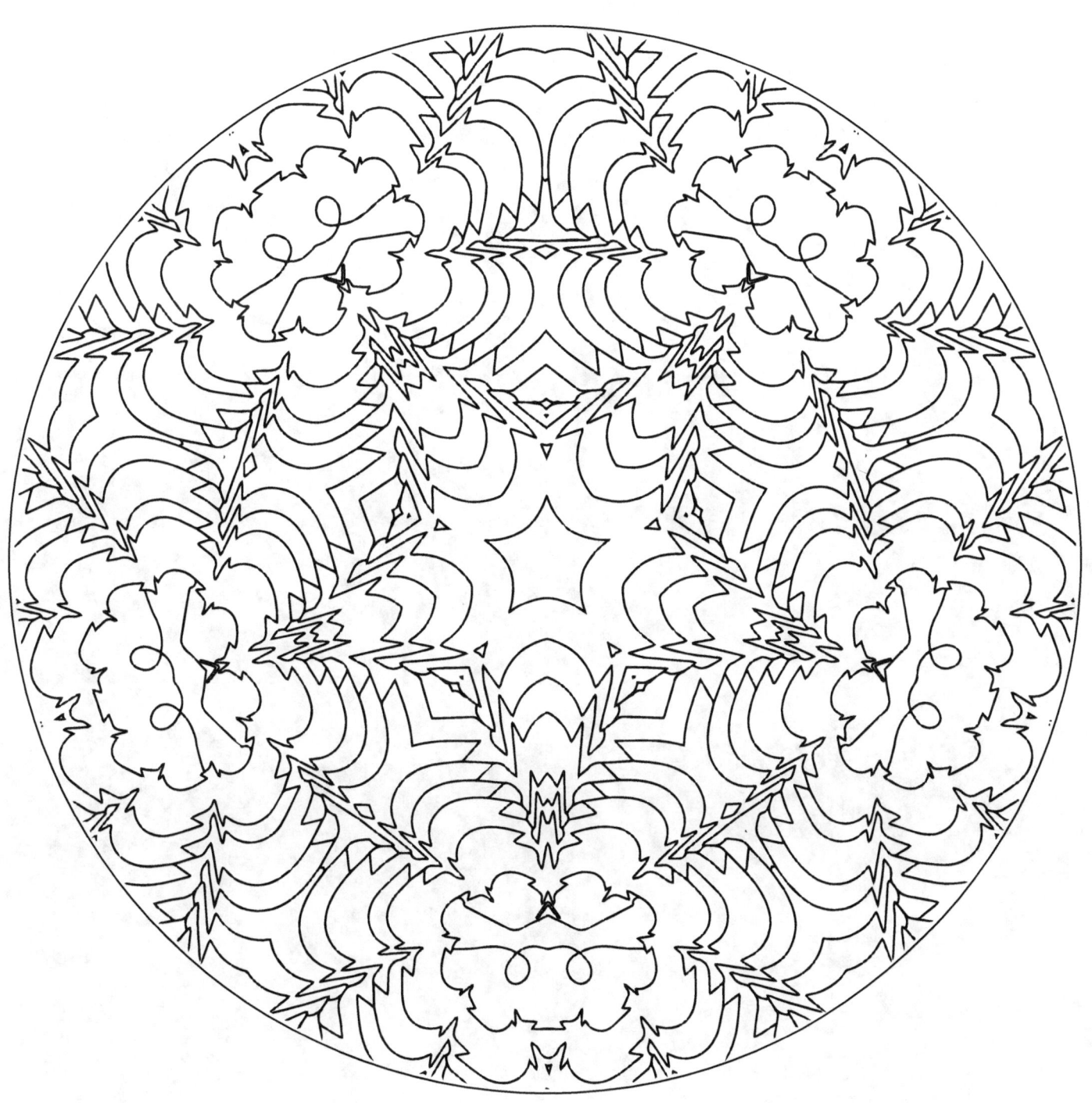

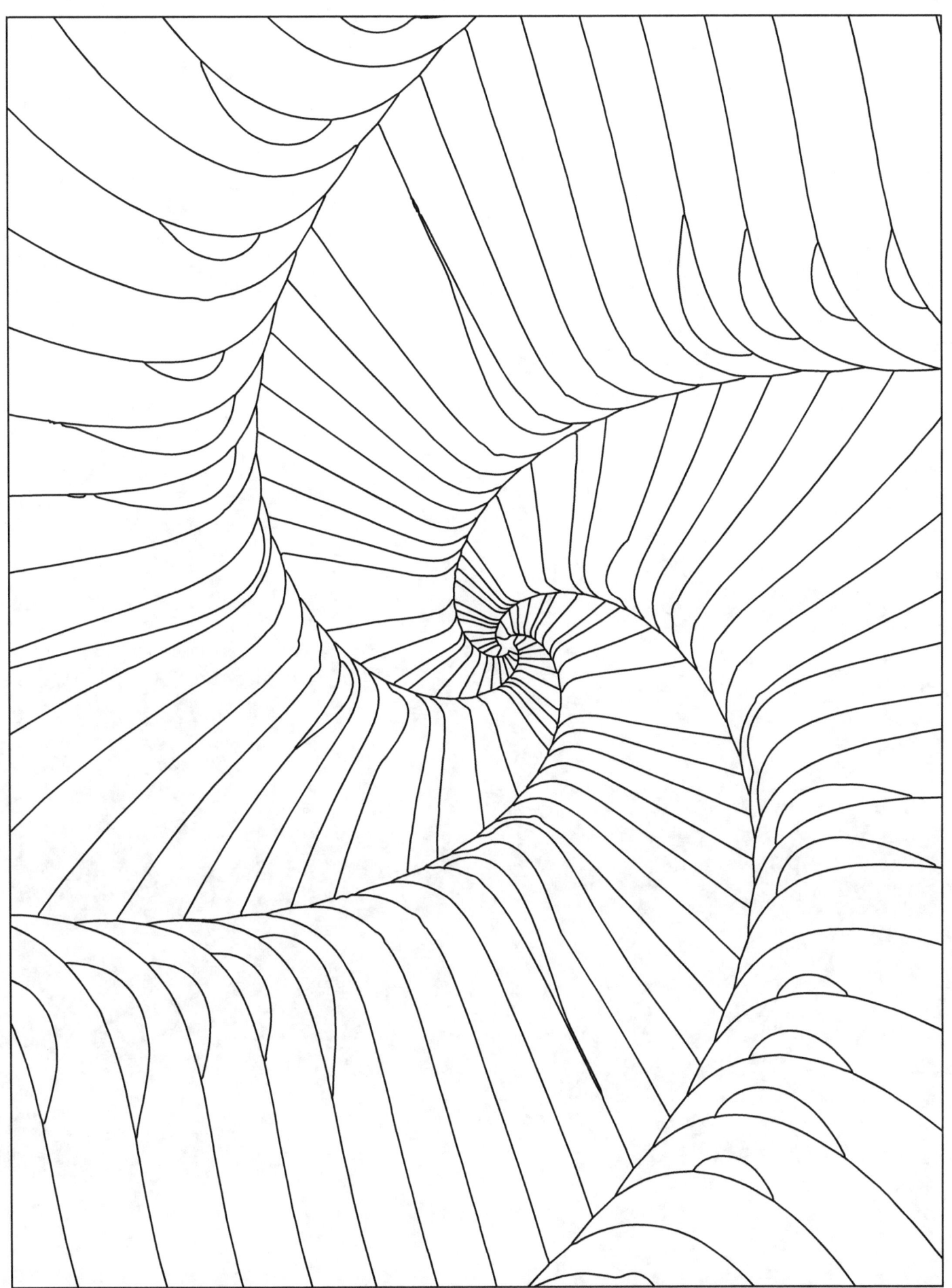

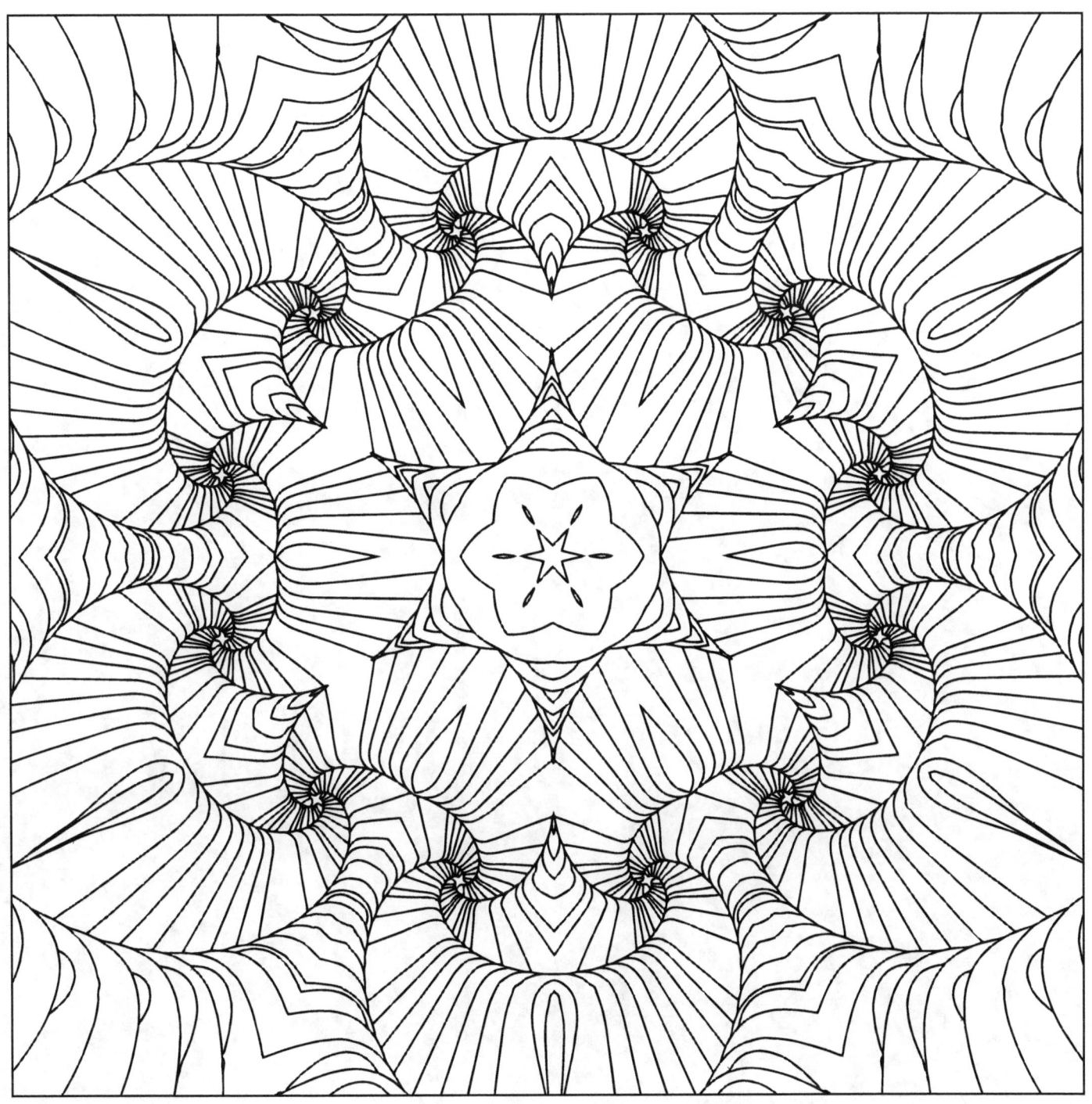

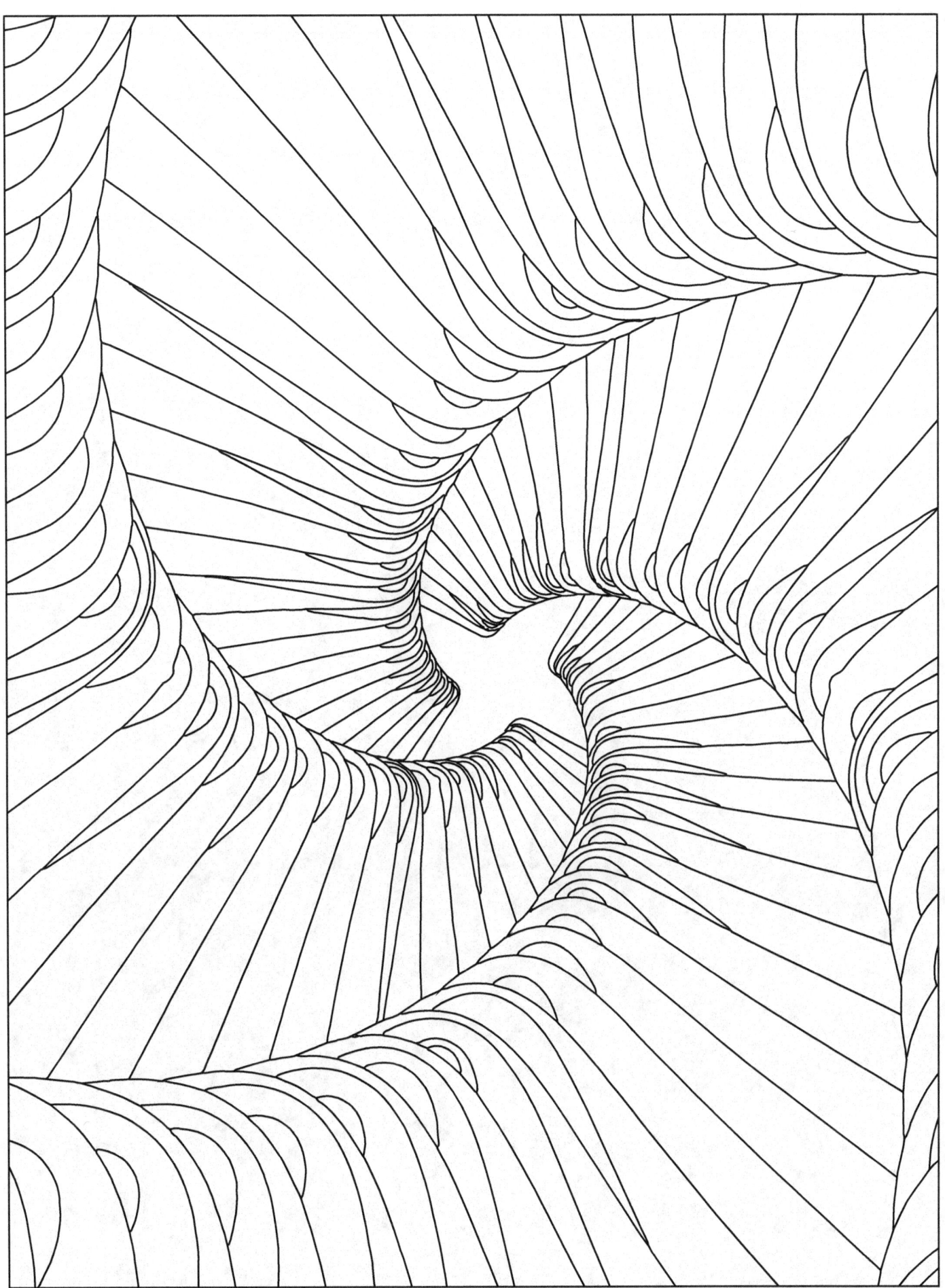

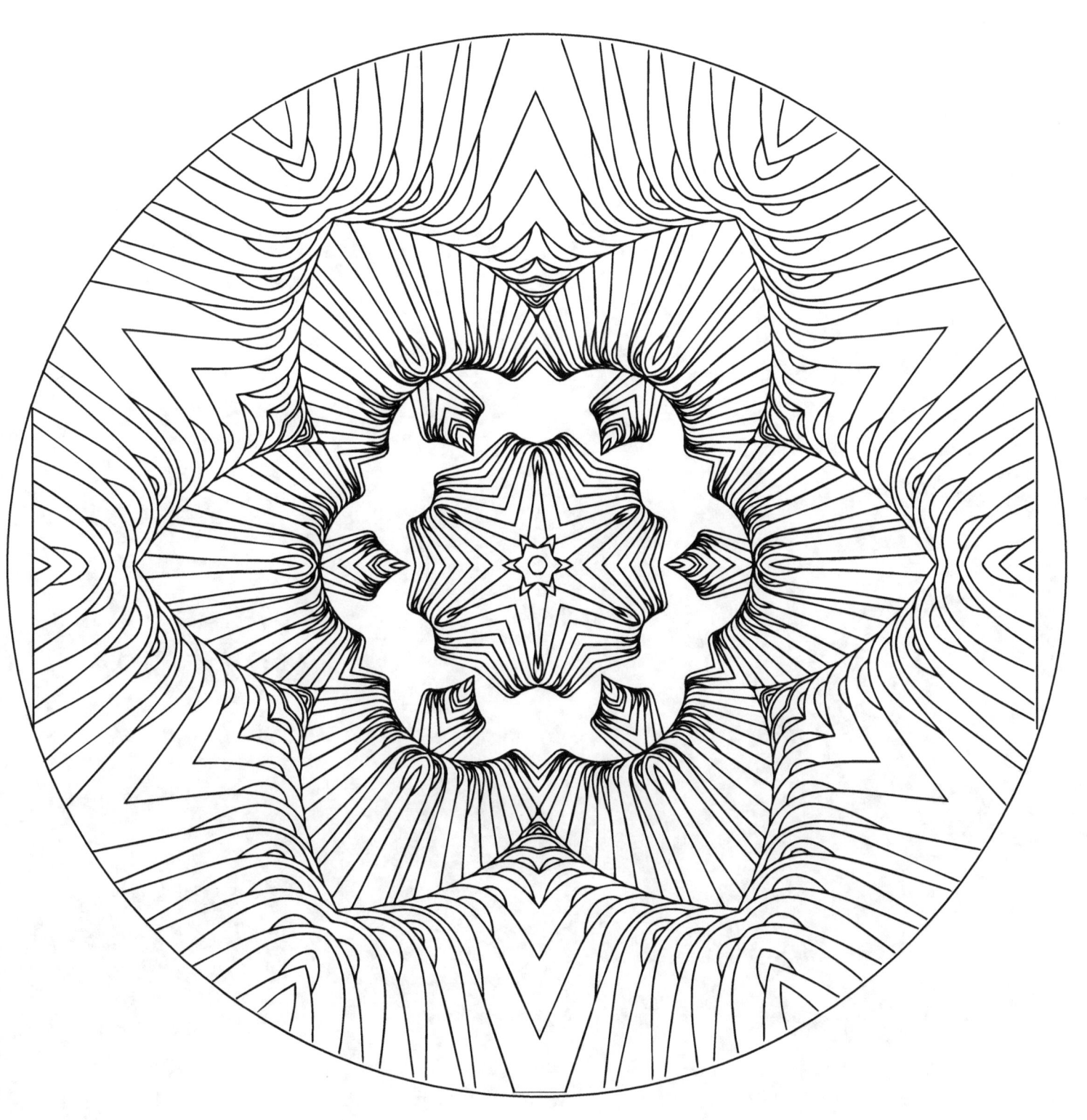

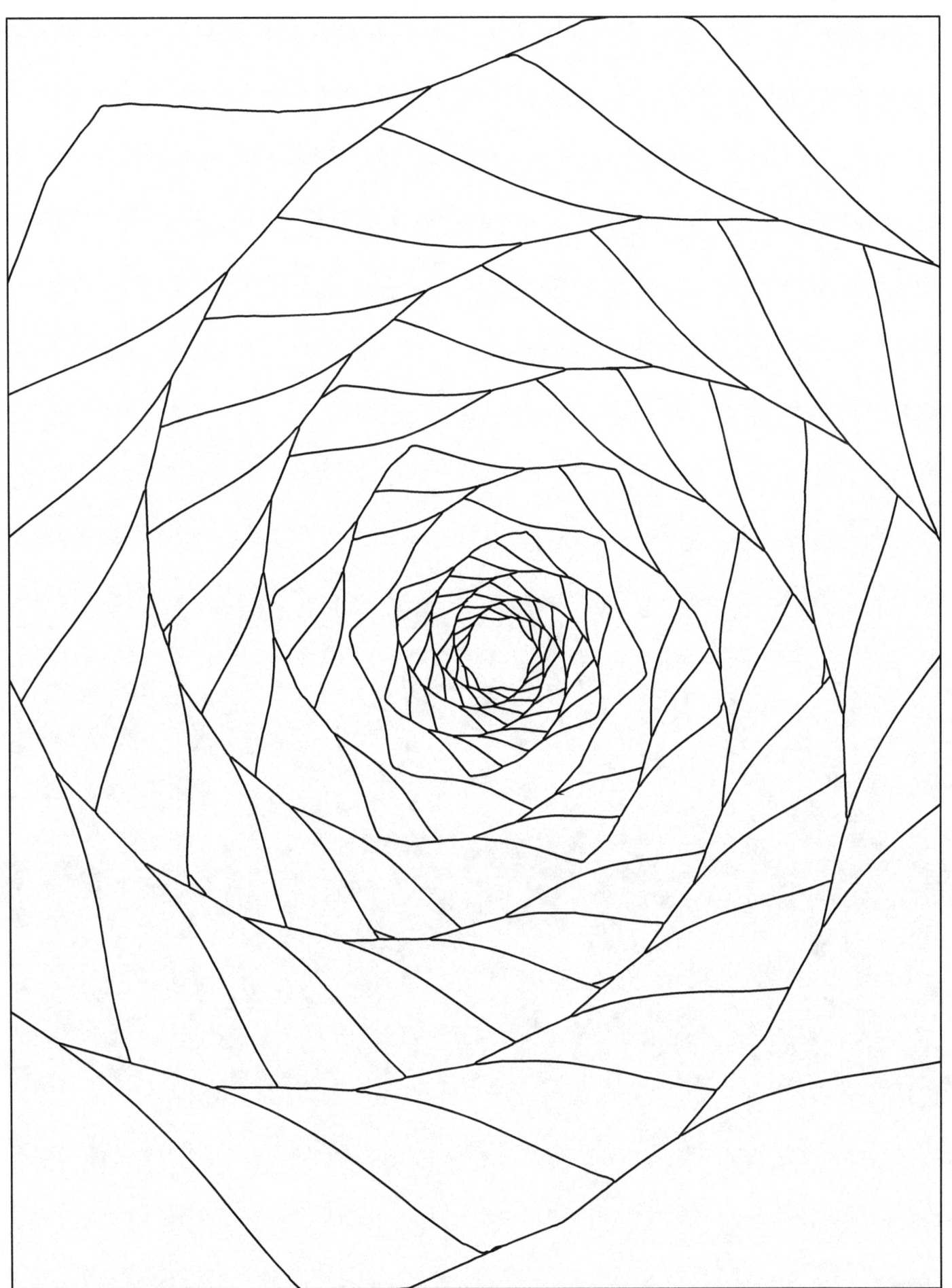

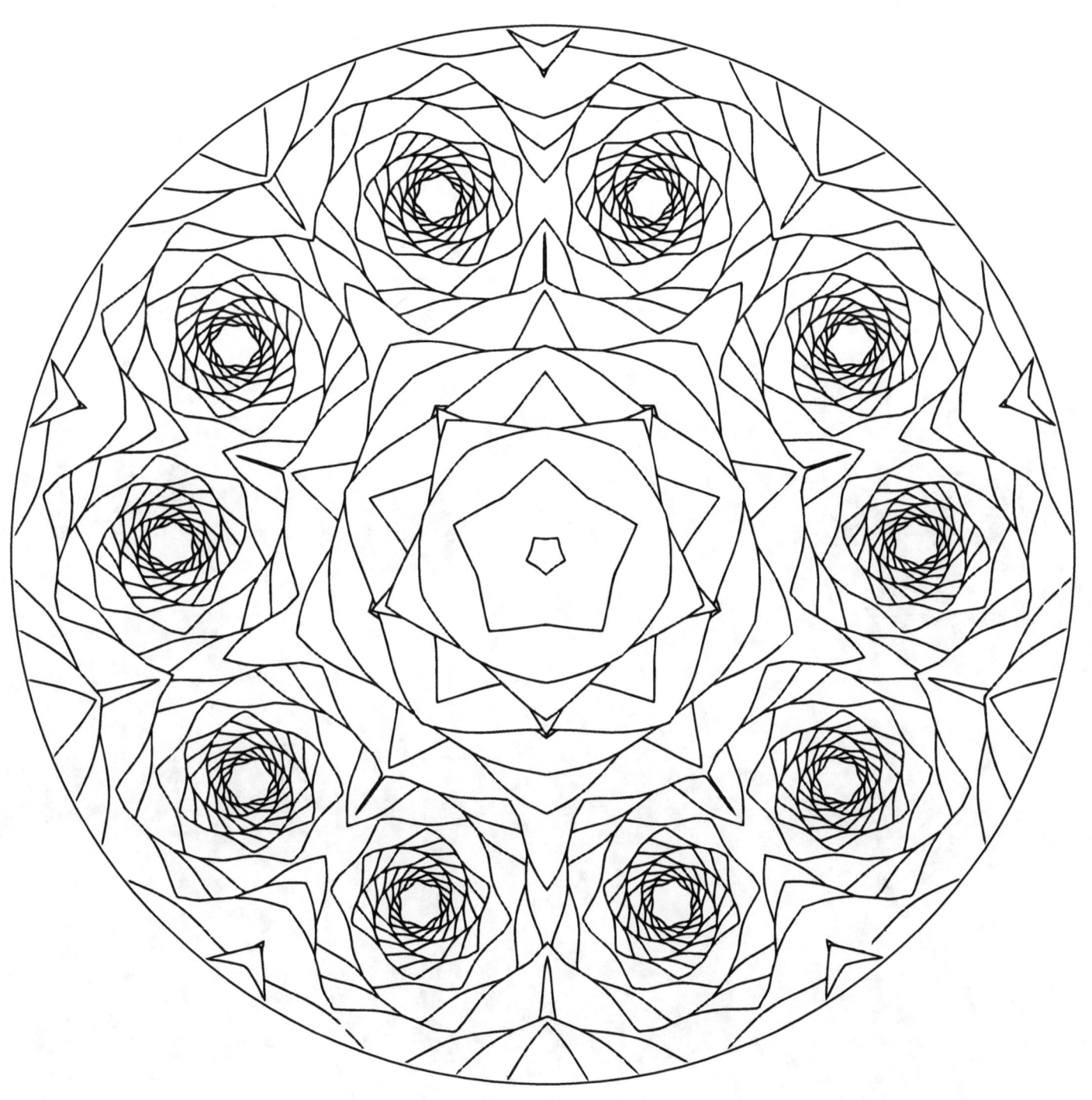

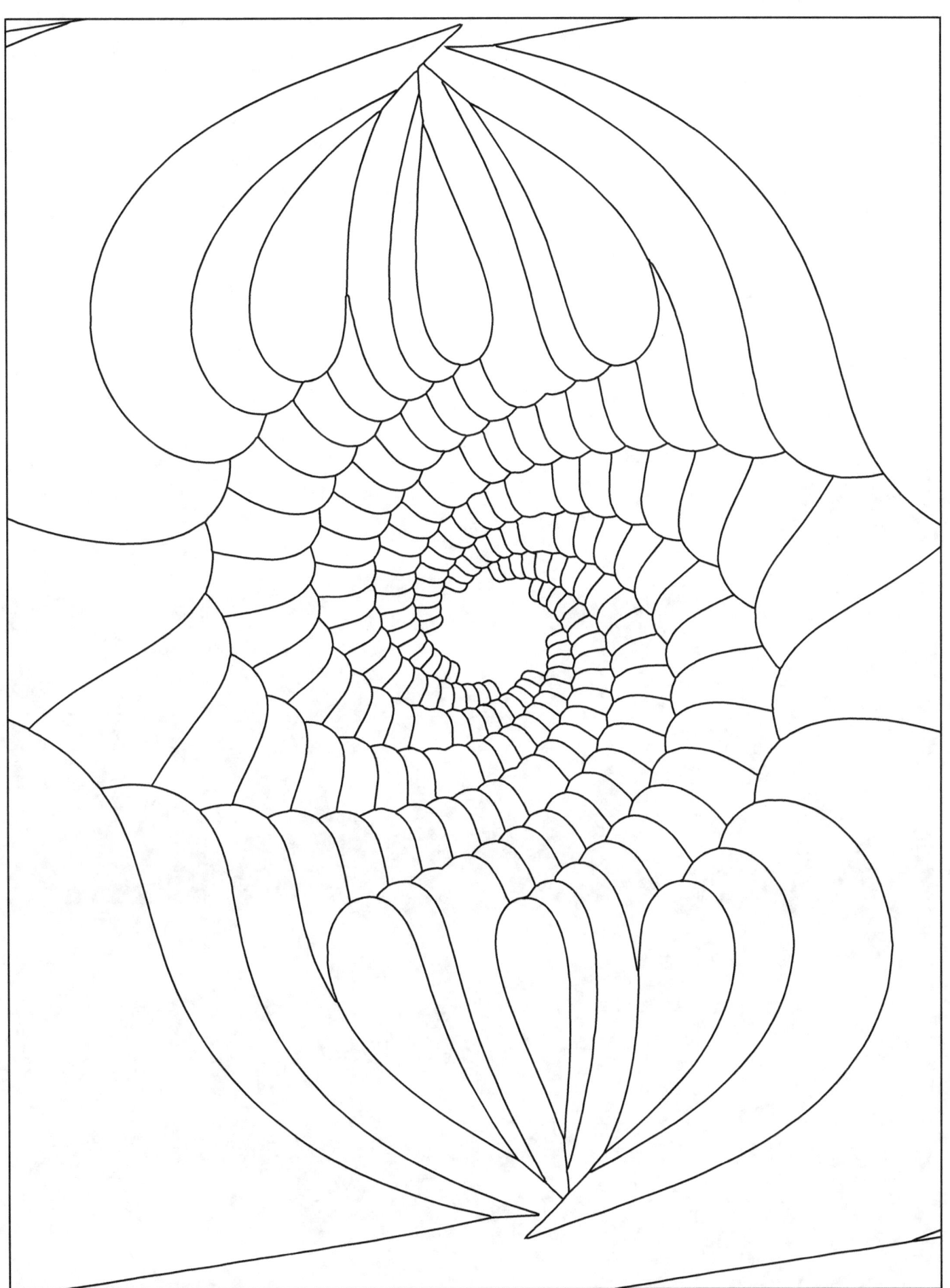

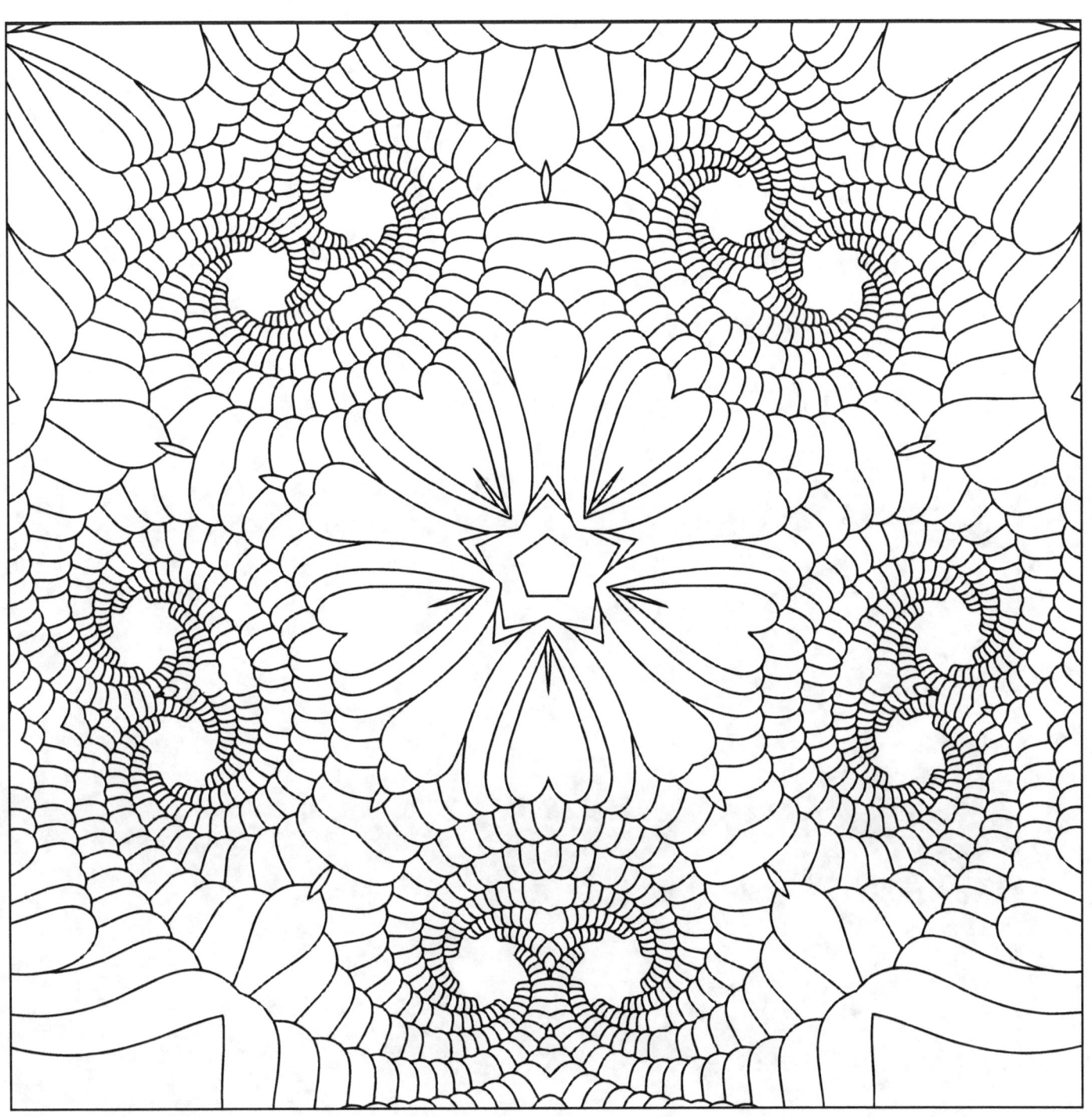

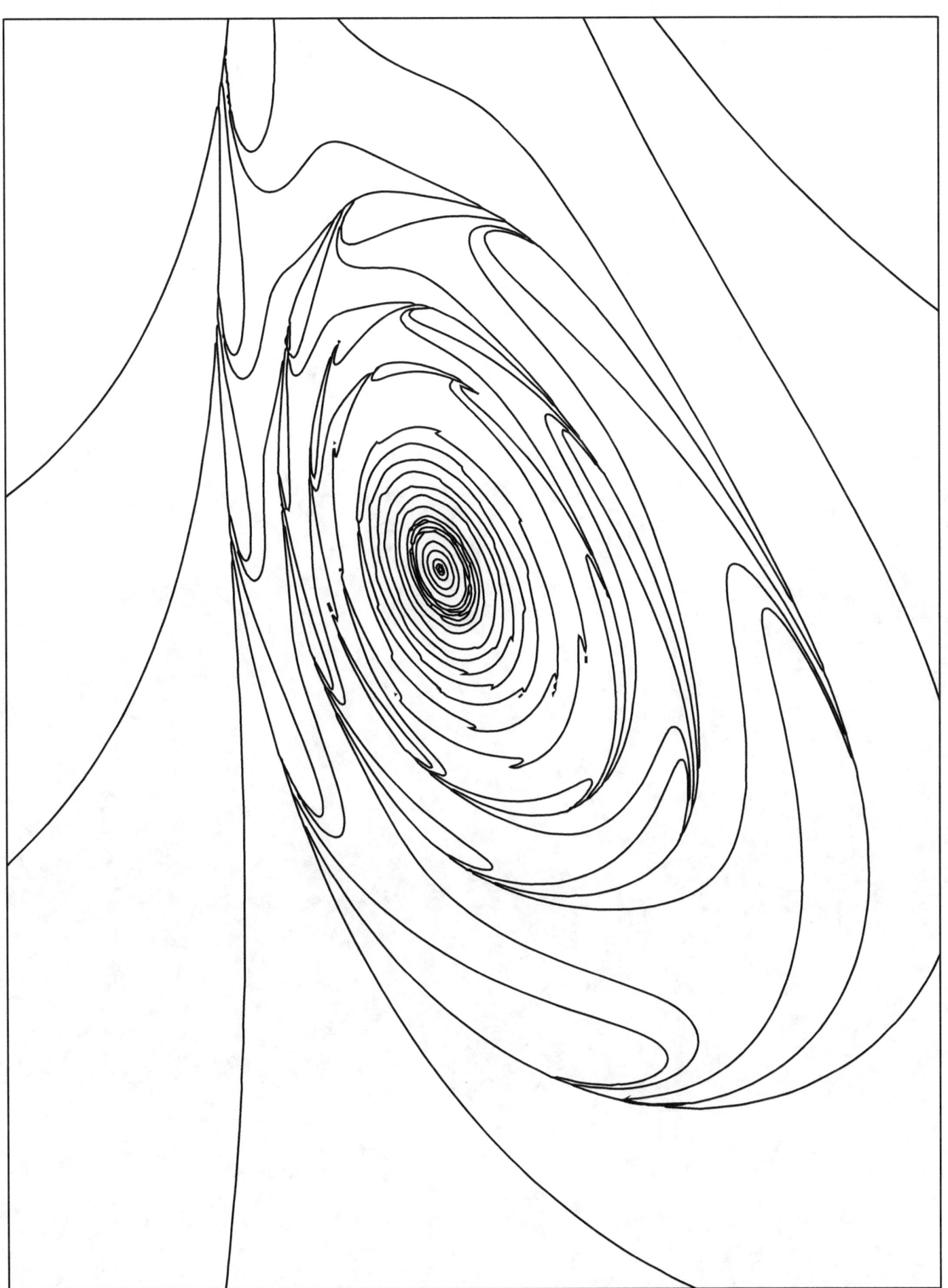

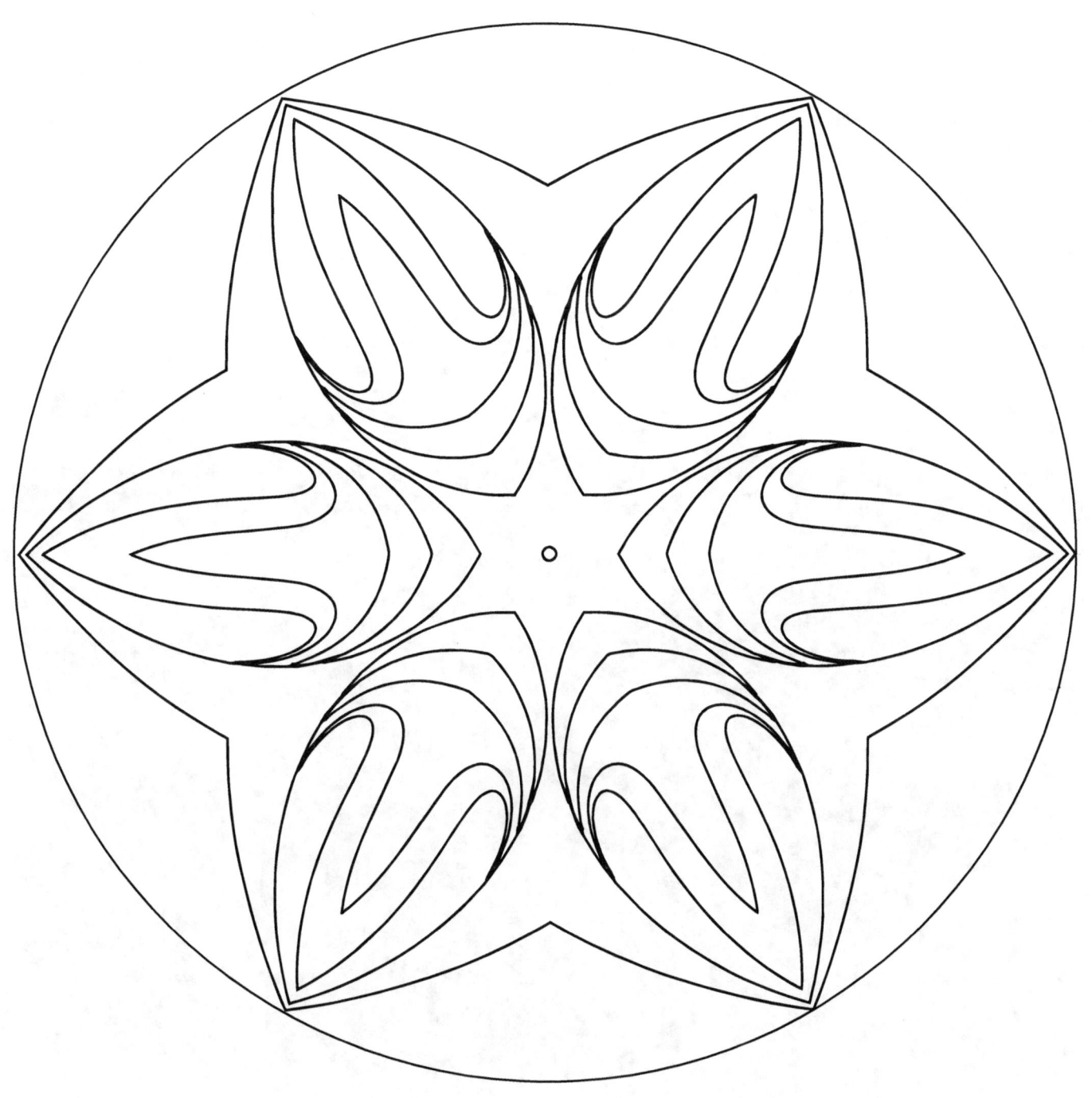

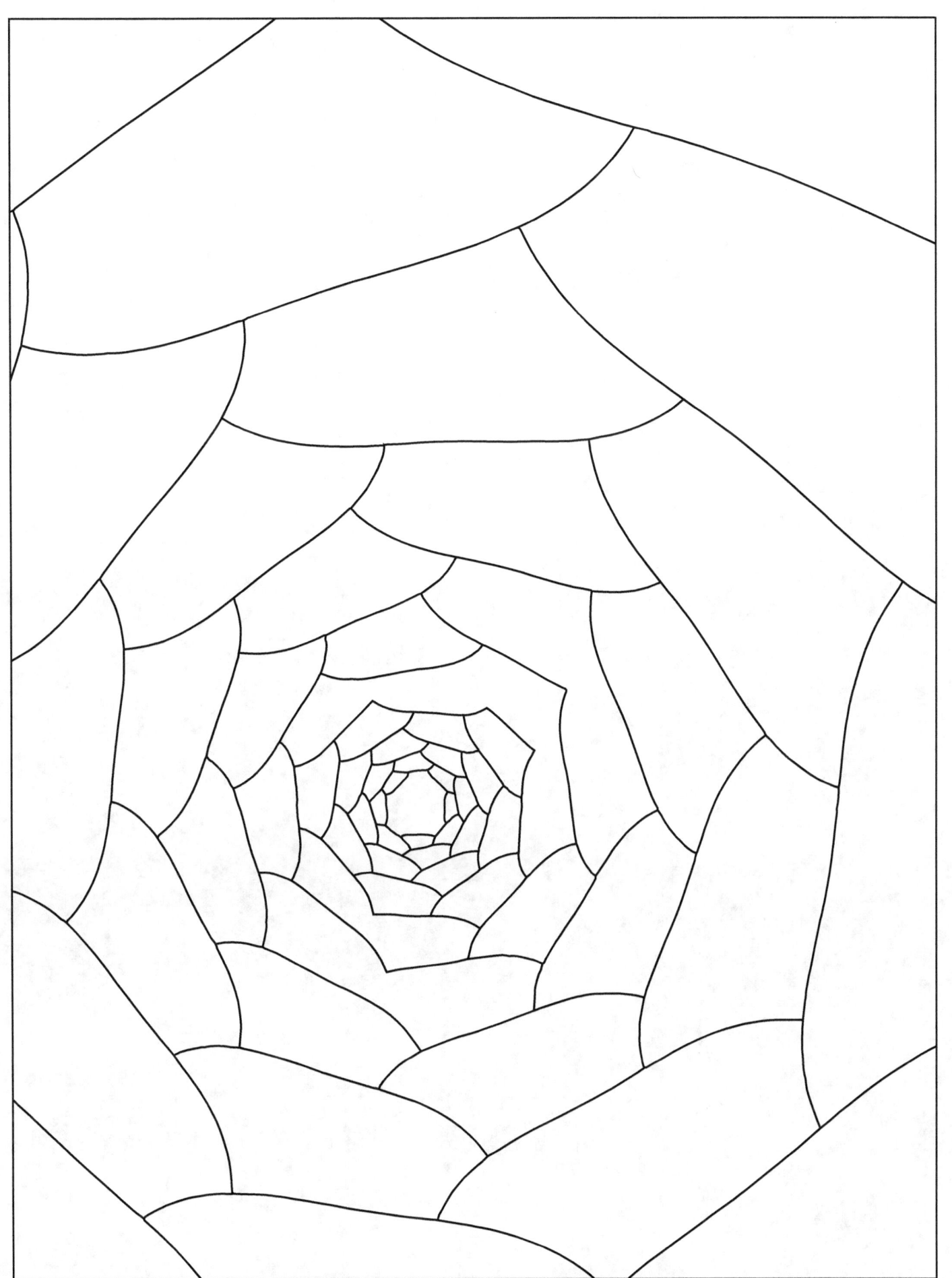

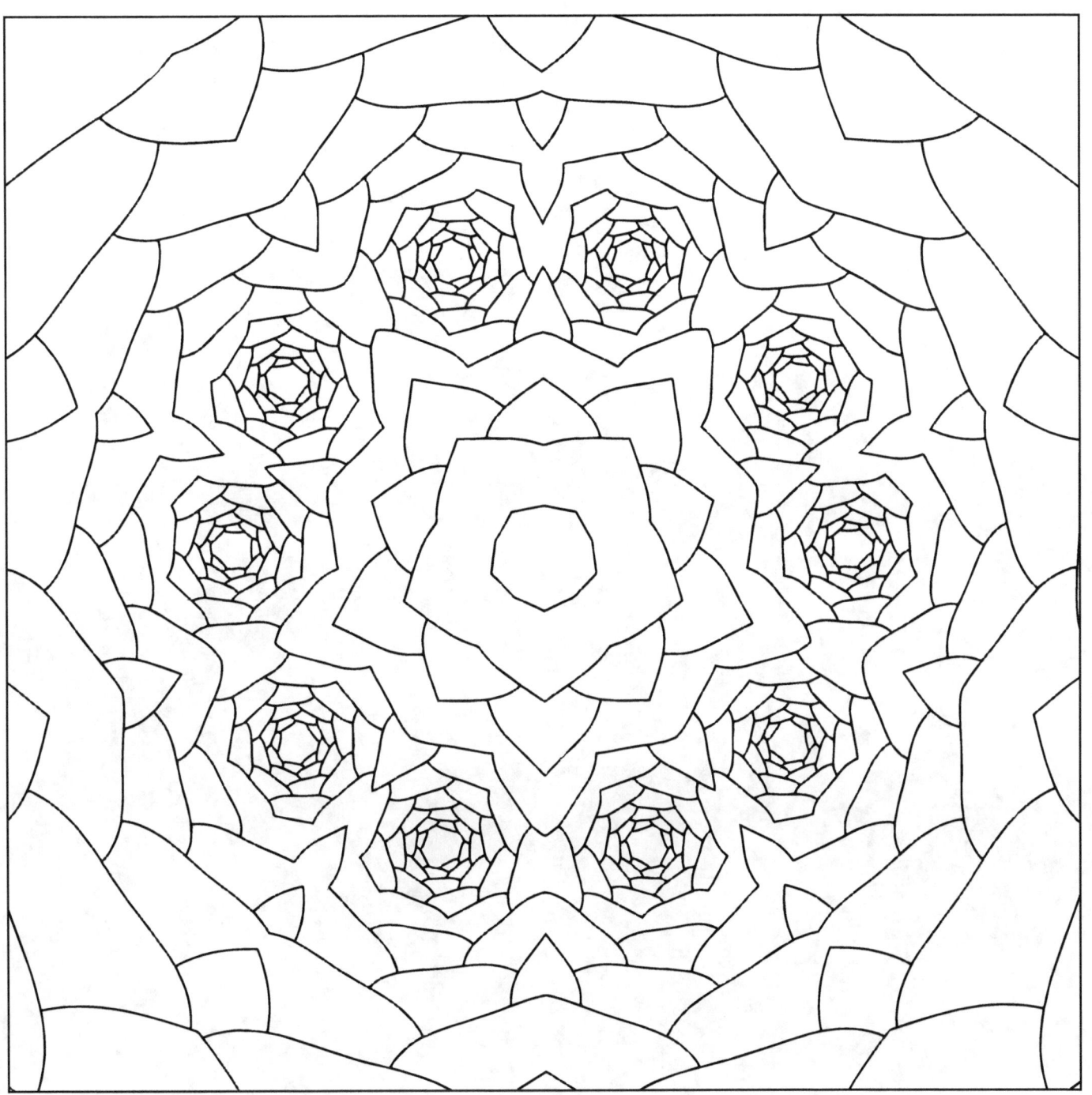

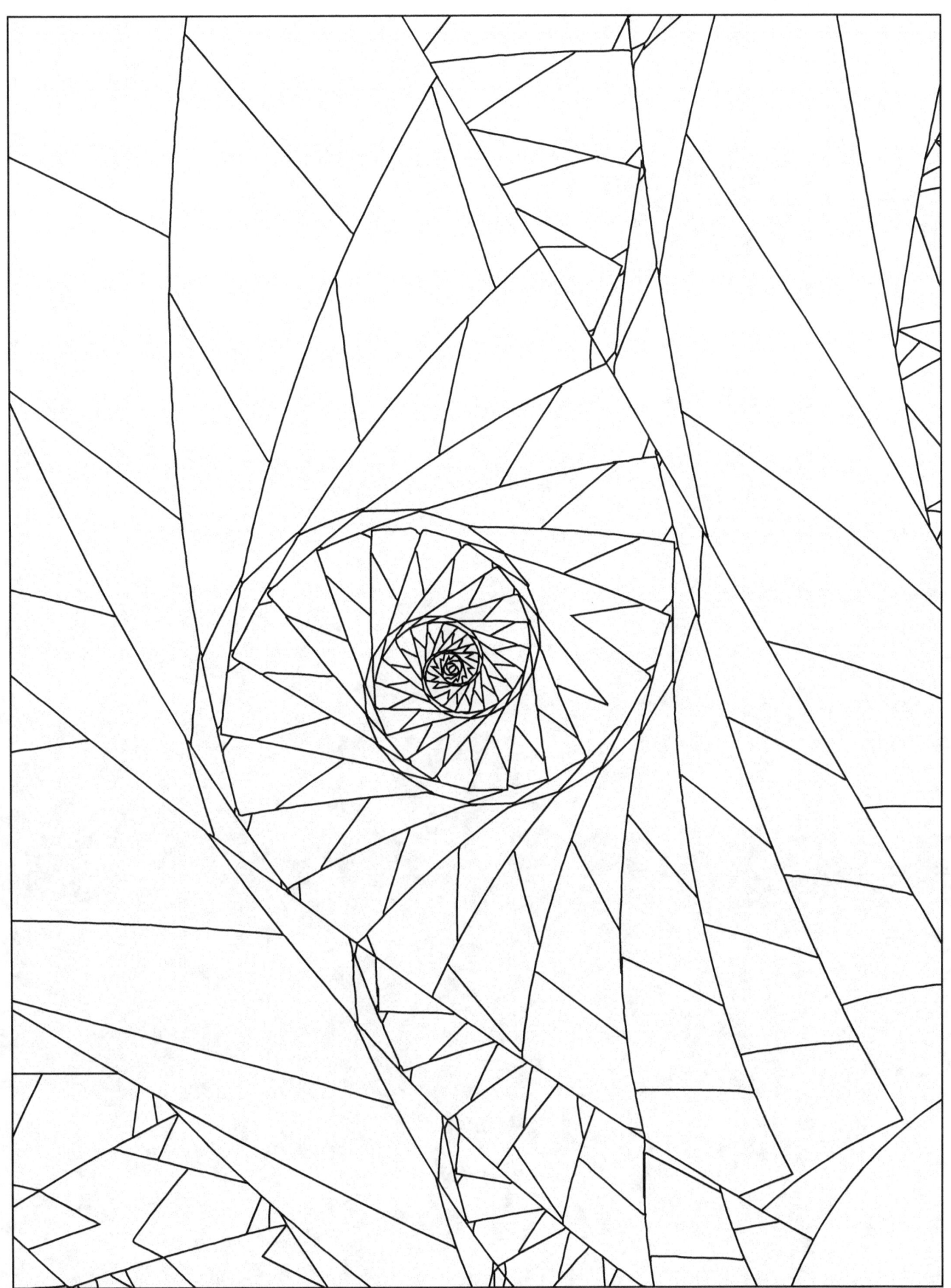

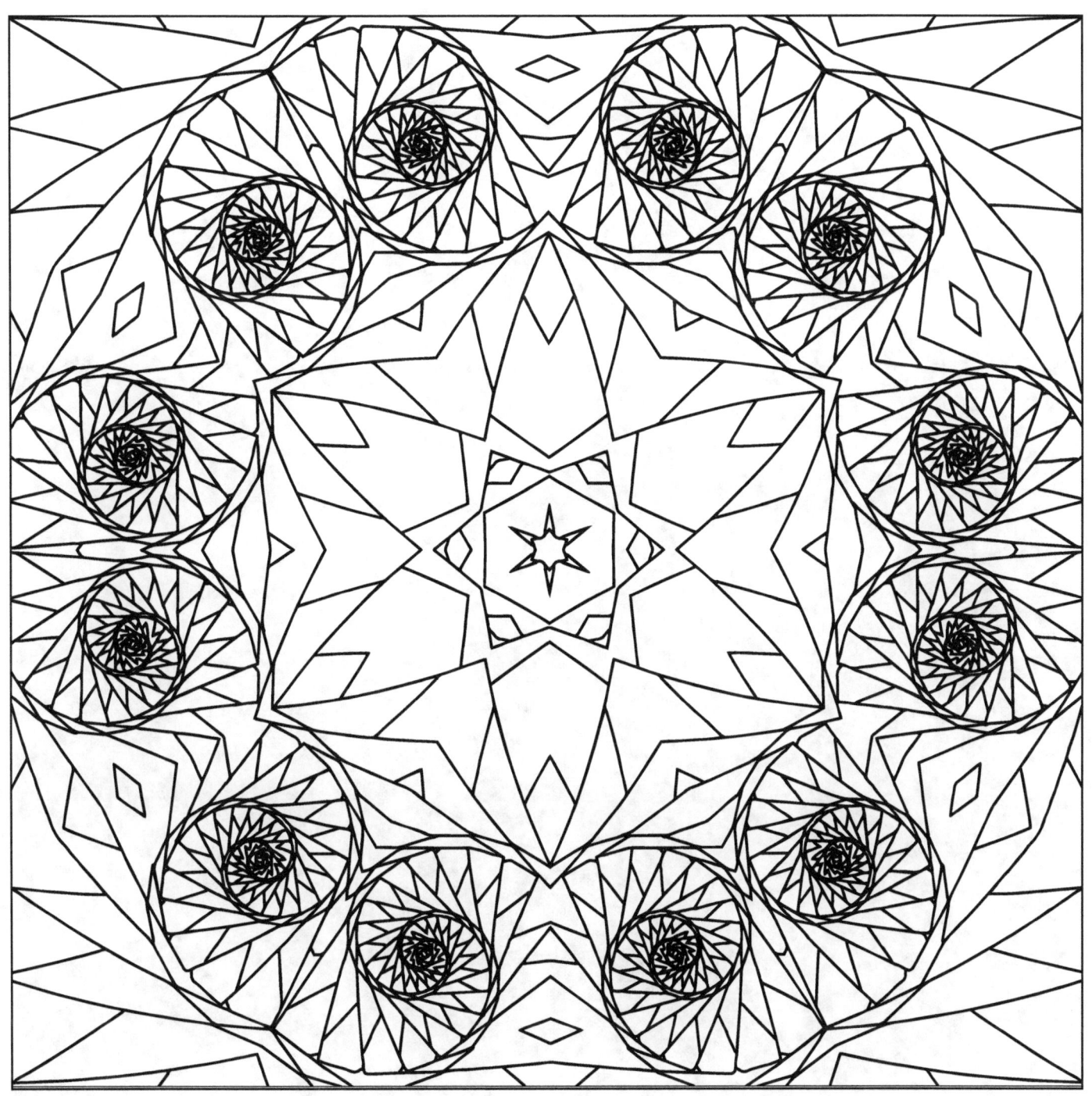

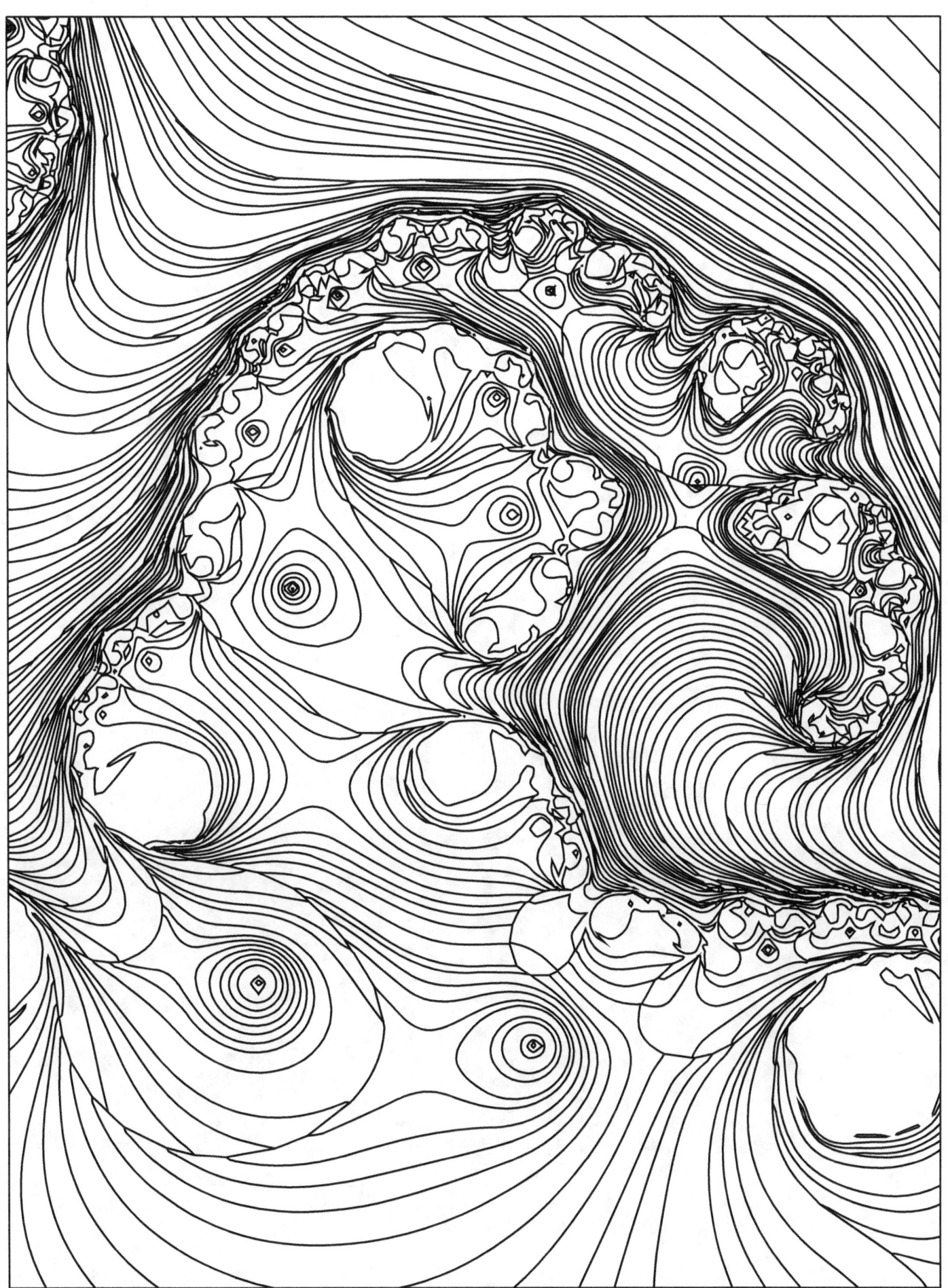

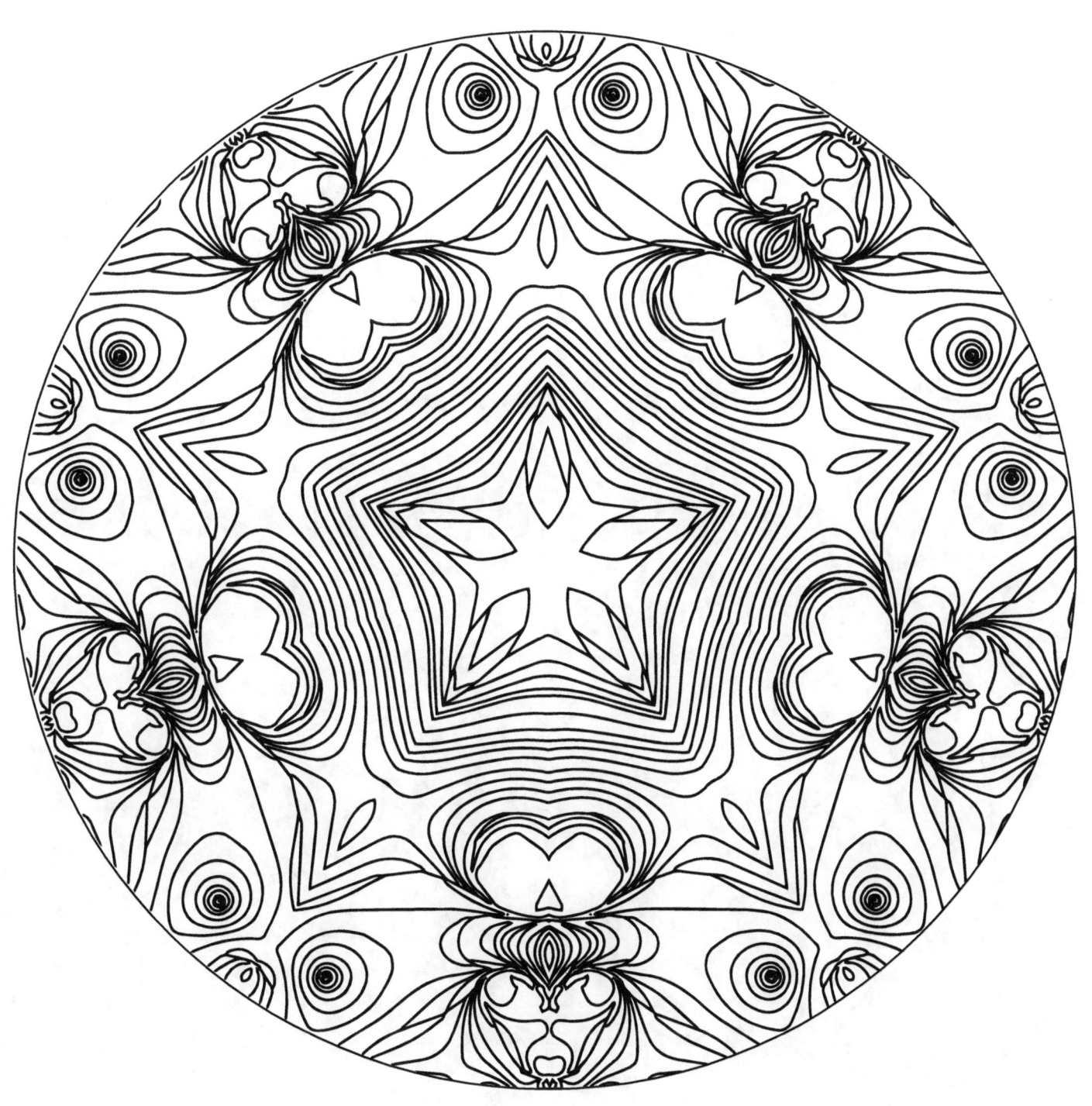

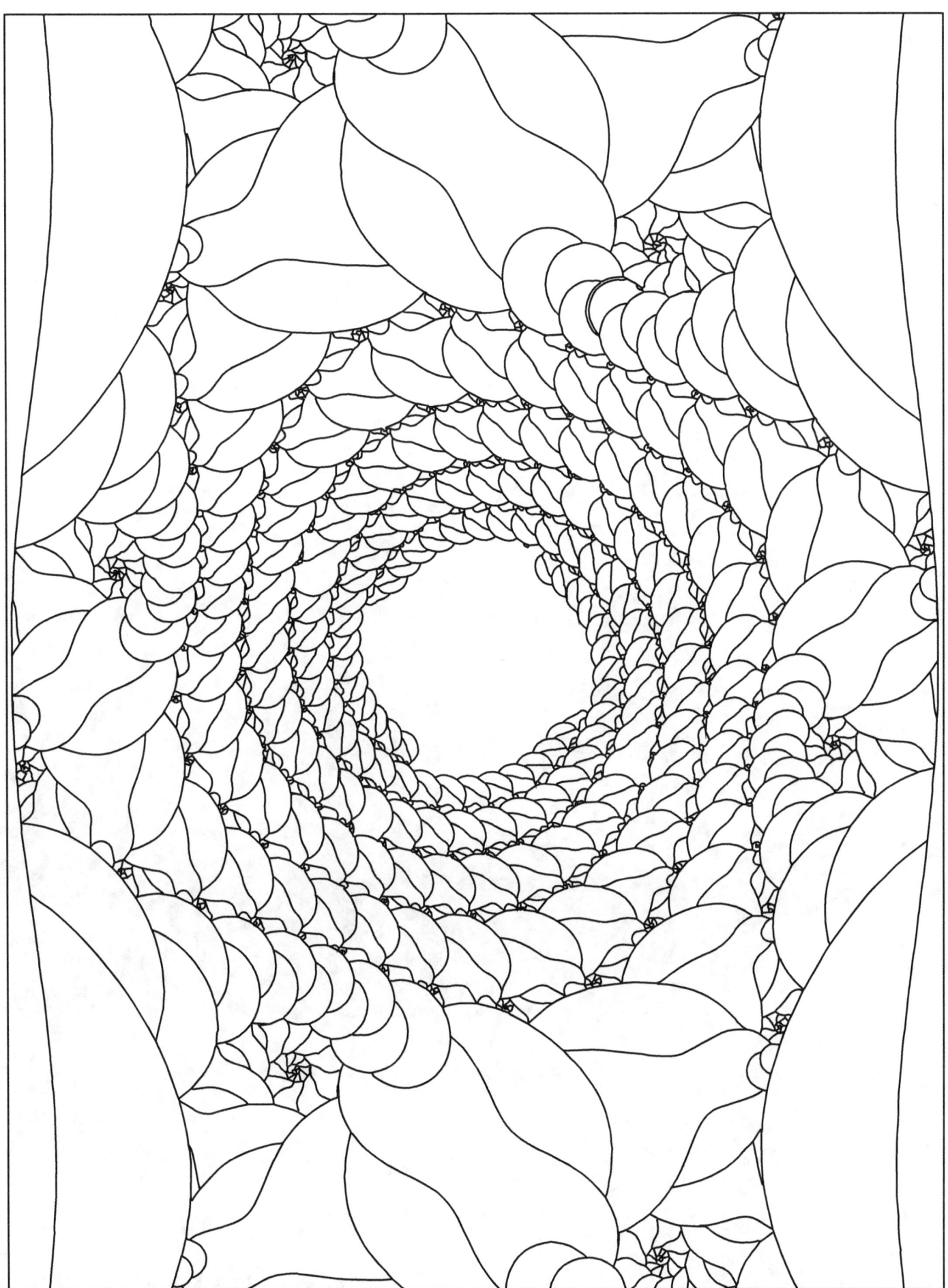

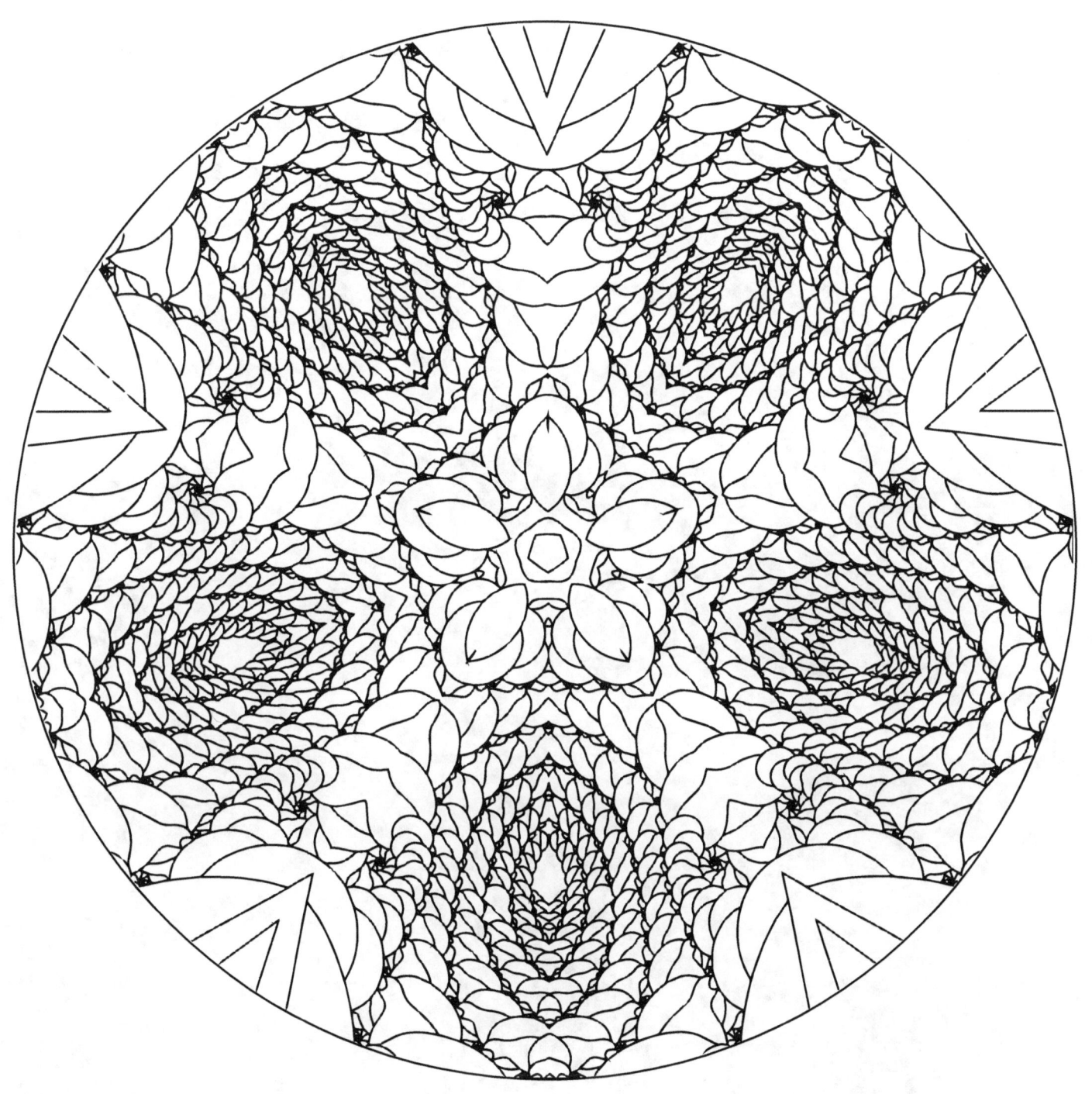

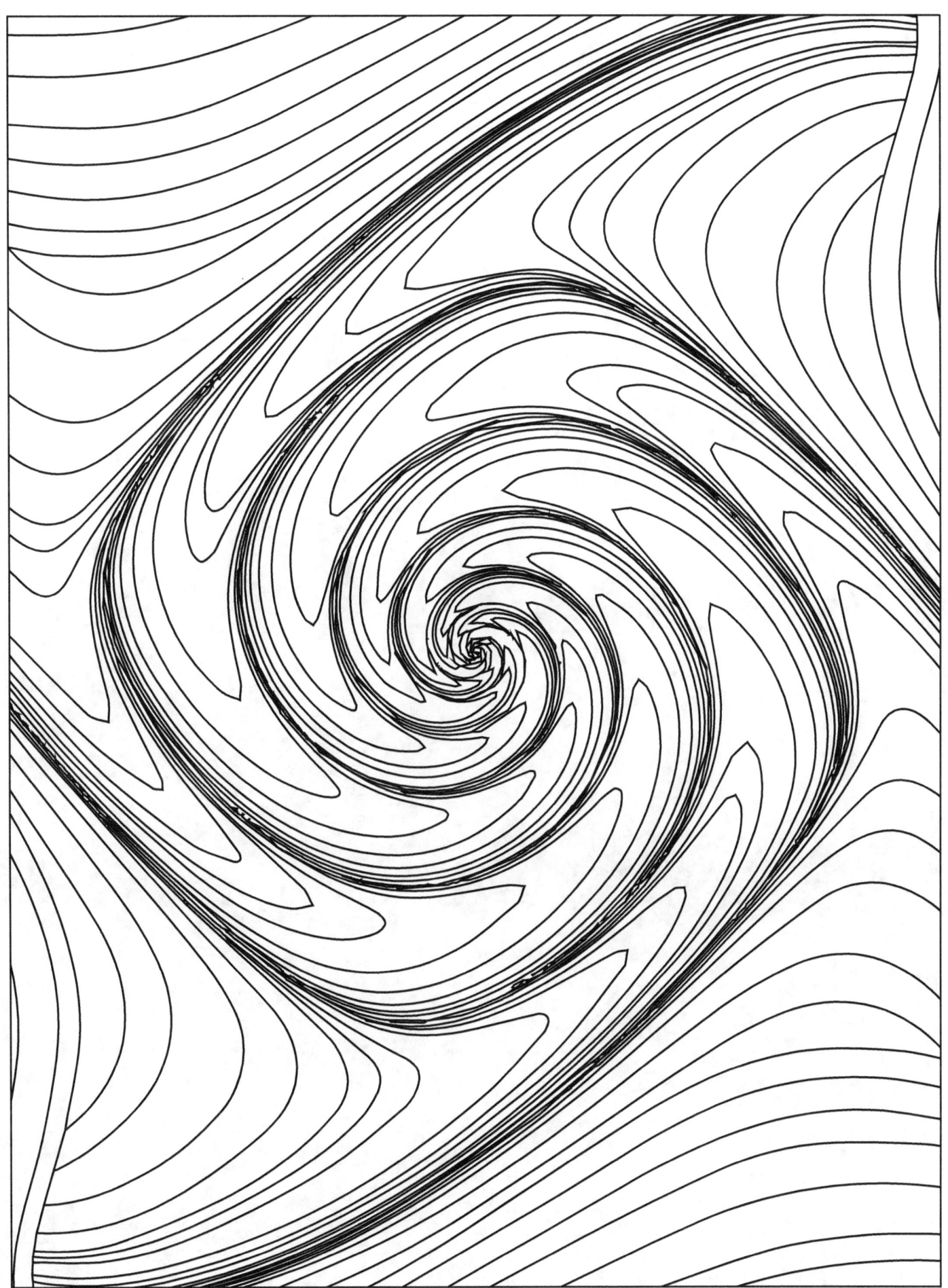

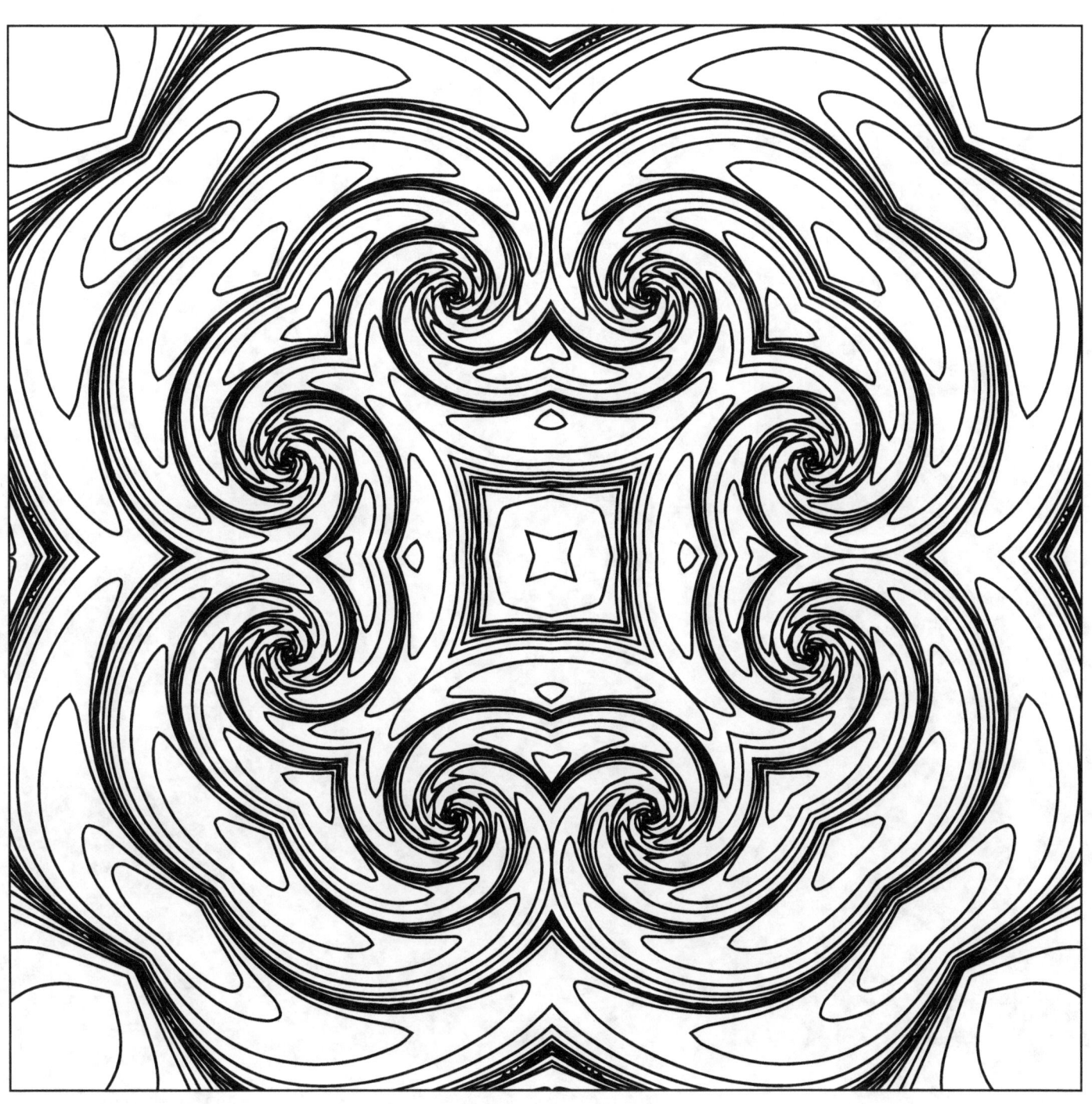

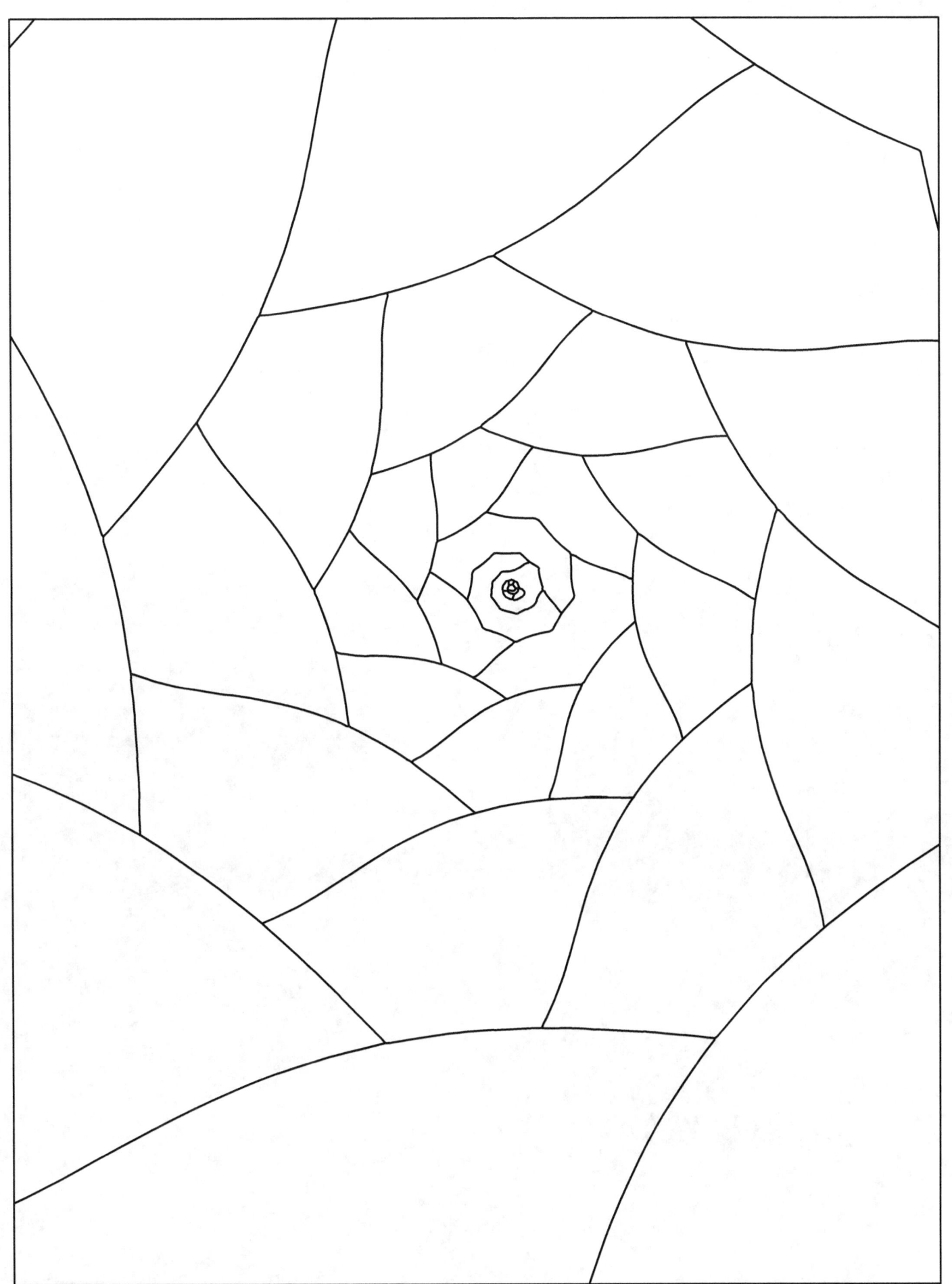

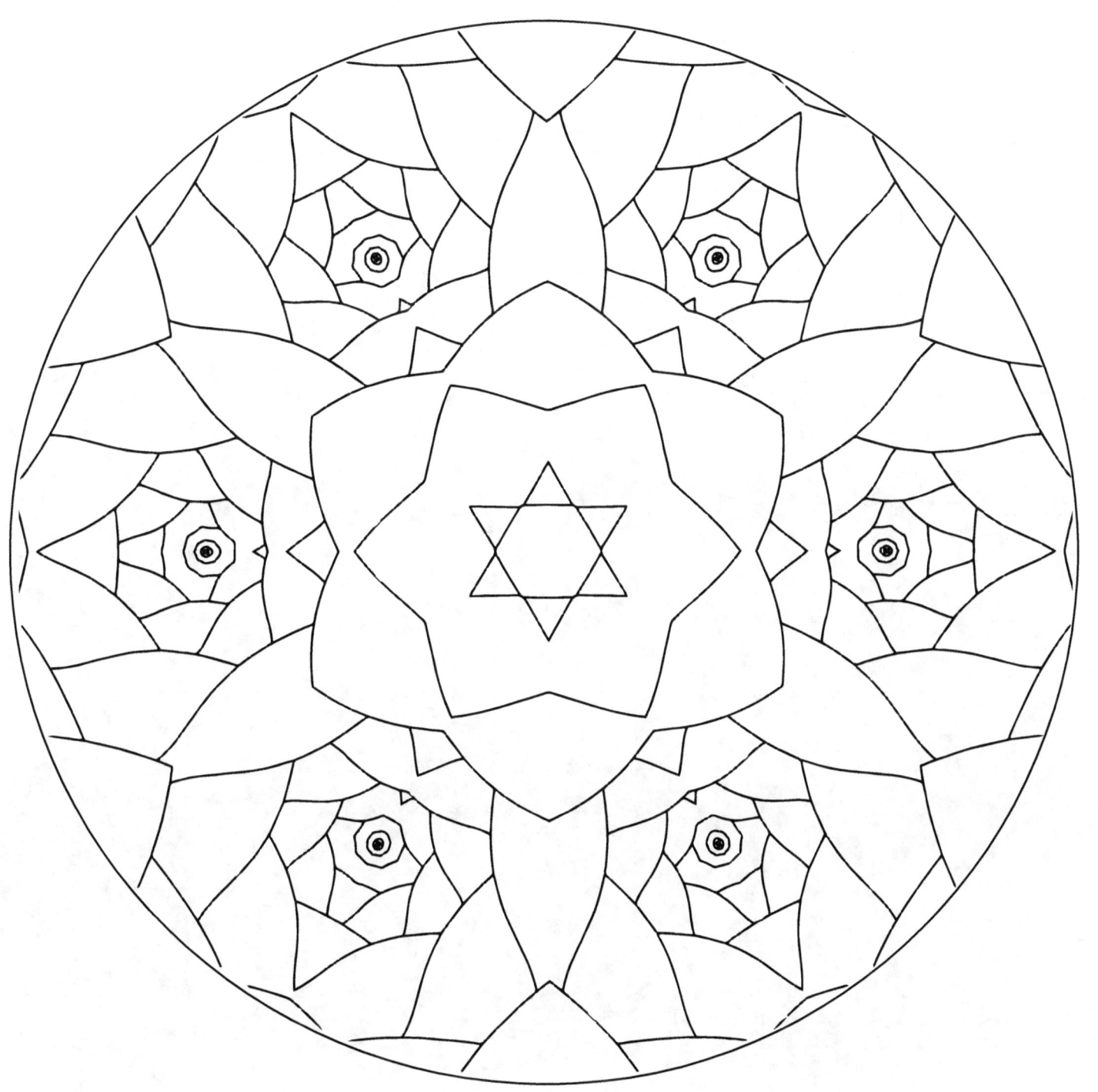

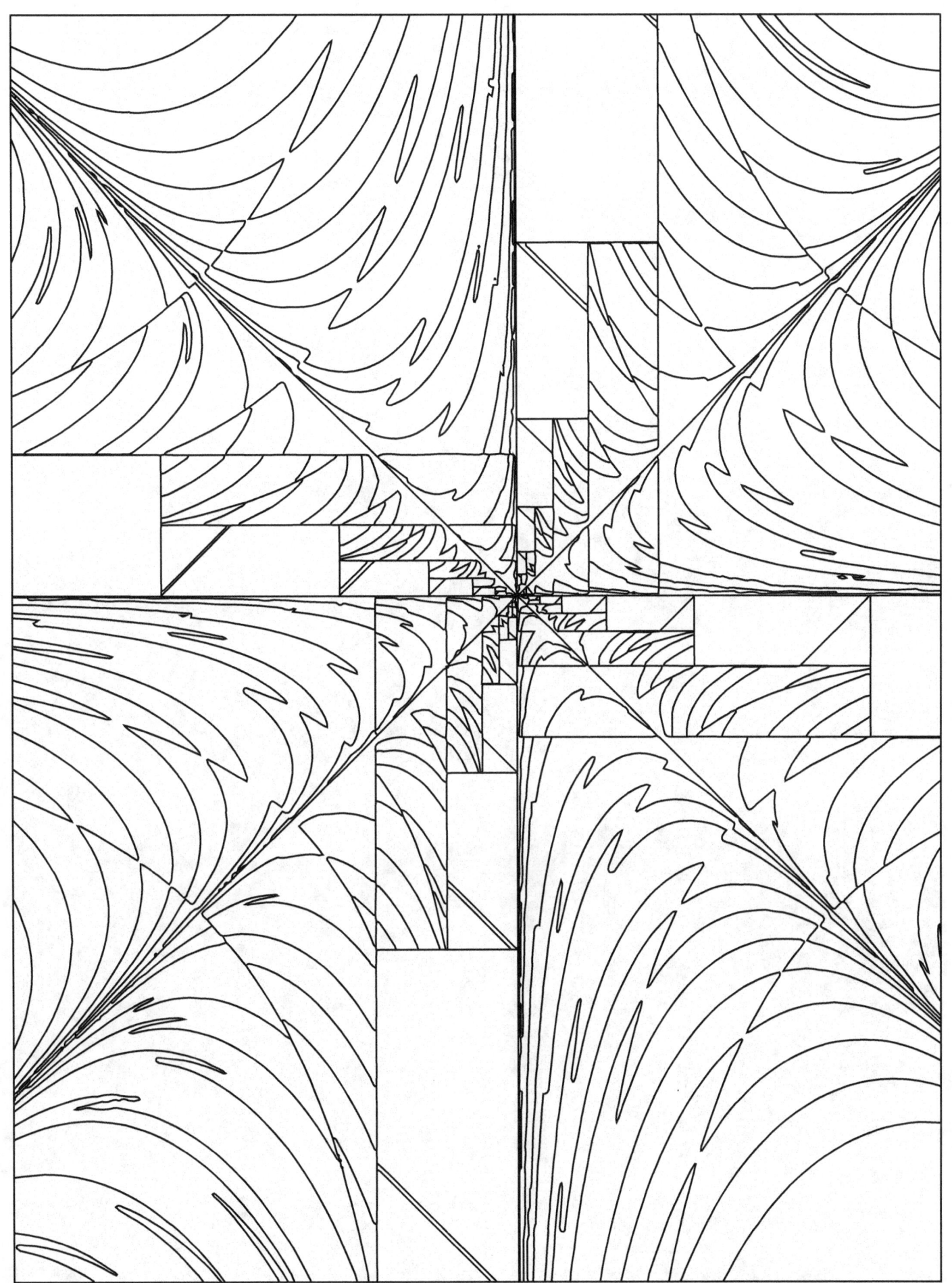

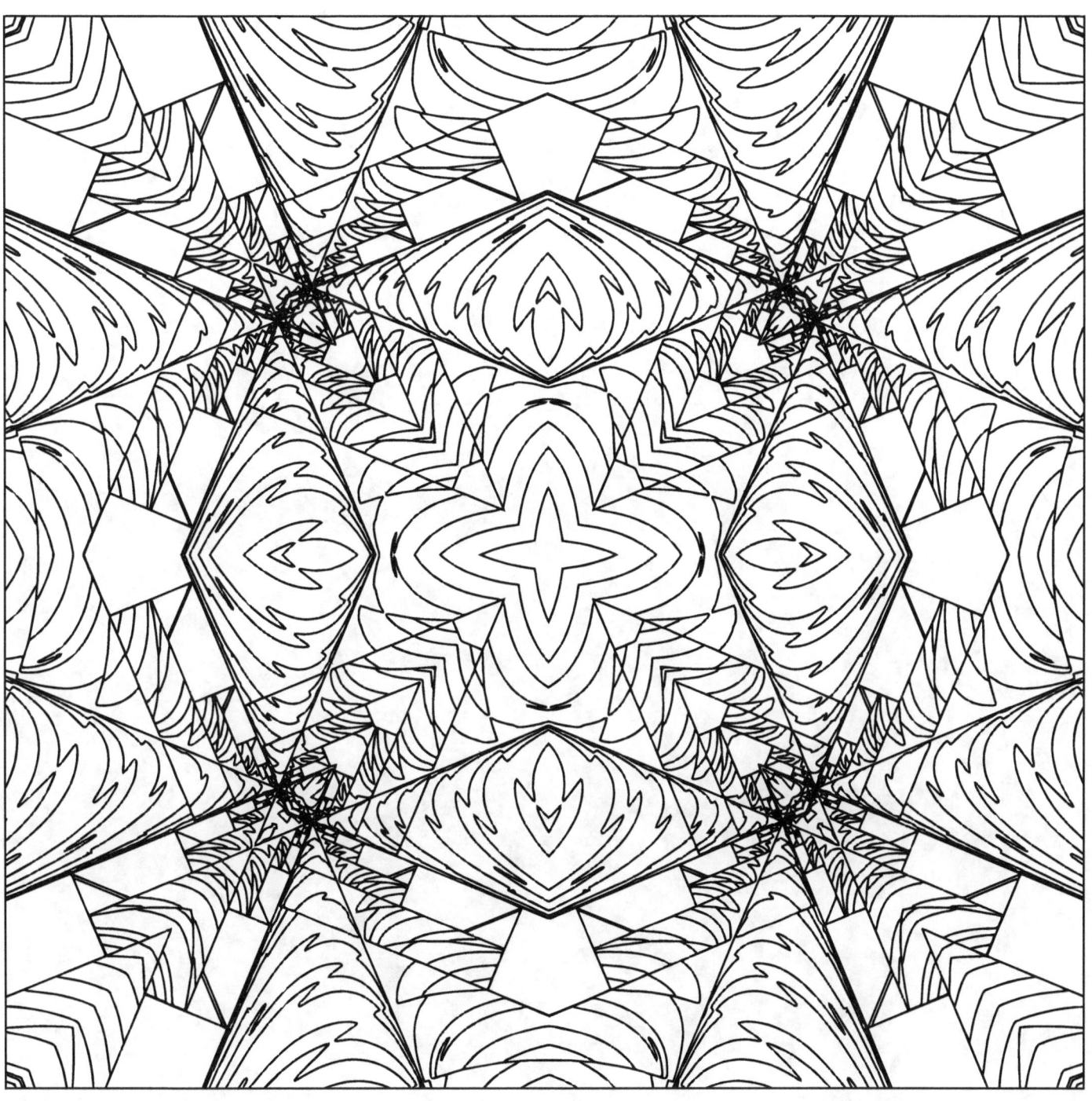

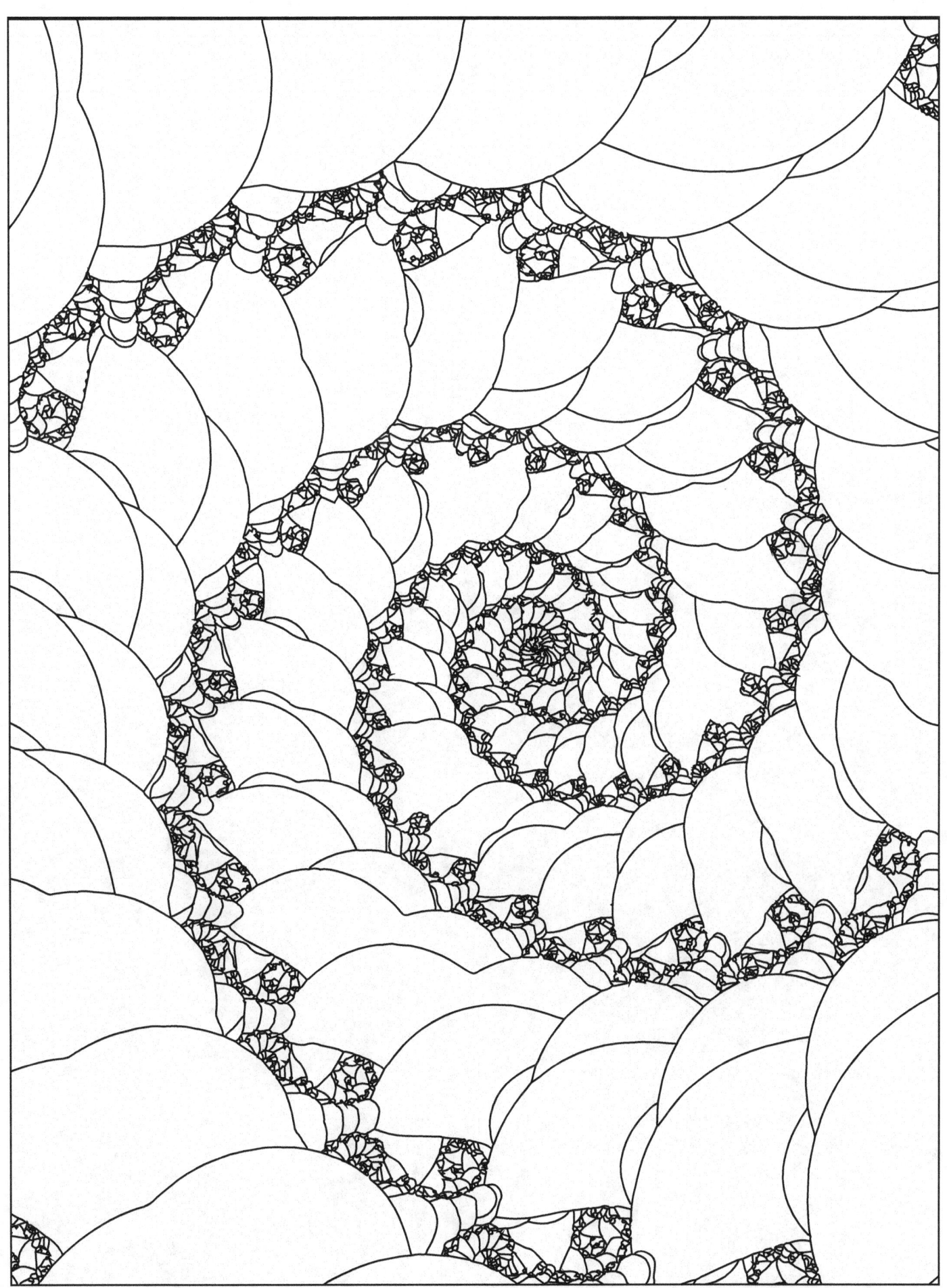

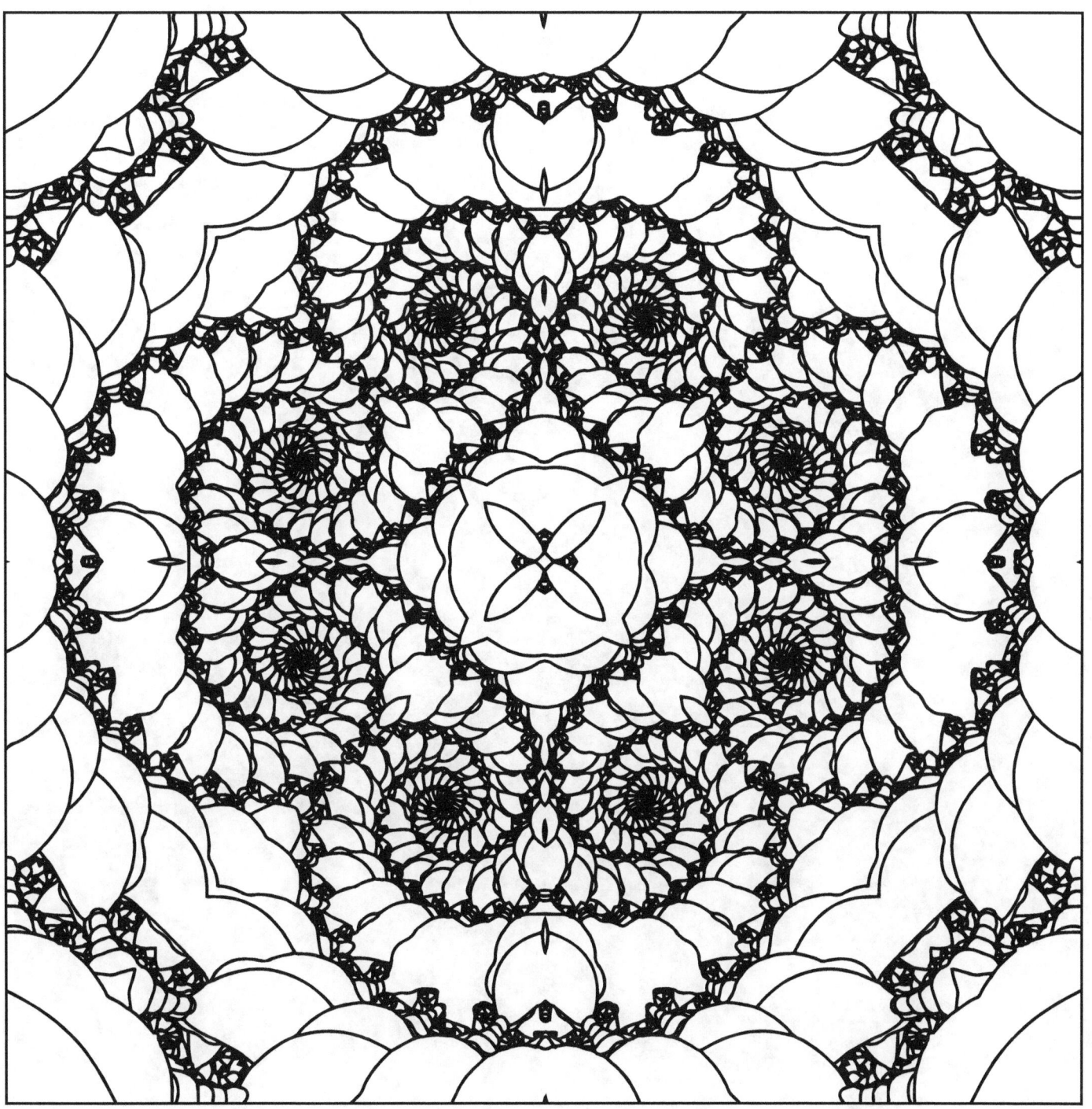